FOREWORD

Henderson's Relish has been made in Sheffield since 1885. Nearly 140 years later, we remain an independent family business and we're still mixing and bottling Sheffield's famous sauce with its secret recipe.

It has long been thought that Henderson's Relish is only available in Sheffield. As if Hendo's is our secret! Many who move here discover Henderson's Relish for the first time, and Sheffielders who move away make regular trips home to buy a bottle or two, thinking they can't get it anywhere else.

Back in 1981, the Sheffield Star visited our famous old factory on Leavygreave Road. The mischievous 79-year-old managing director, Neville Freeman, told the young reporter that "if you mention Henderson's Relish in Rotherham, they don't know what you're talking about." But Mr Freeman couldn't resist showing off his little red book of export orders too: gallons going to Winnipeg, Brisbane, and O'Sullivan Beach, places where postage was three times the cost of the Relish itself.

Over the years, the Henderson's business has grown, and our brand name has become well known across the UK, and around the world. Today, its distinctive orange labels adorn the shelves of supermarkets and independent stores from Broomhall to Buenos Aires. Recently, I answered a customer enquiry from a gentleman in Mexico; apparently, they put an English sauce (I didn't recognise the name) on pizza over there, and he was very excited to find Henderson's Relish — the best 'Salsa Inglesa' he'd ever tasted.

For all this, Henderson's Relish has no prouder honour than being Made in Sheffield: our home, known around the world for the quality of its work and the warmth of its welcome. Like many of our city's most famous exports, Henderson's Relish brings the best of Sheffield to the world.

In this, our latest book, recipes from around the world are brought to the comfort of your kitchen, as talented friends and followers present over 80 dishes from six continents. Each one is enhanced by a splash, or more, of Henderson's Relish. I hope you enjoy them.

Matt Davies
General Manager

WELCOME TO HENDO'S VS THE WORLD!

Welcome to Hendo's vs The World, a gastronomic globetrotting tour of Henderson's Relish and all the cuisines it can enhance, complement, and elevate.

Chefs and restaurateurs with heritages from across the globe have developed dishes that balance the unique notes of flavour in Sheffield's favourite condiment with the hallmarks of their cuisine, from South African stew to Malaysian noodles and a bit of everything in between.

We've divided the recipes that follow into chapters based on their place of origin, travelling through six continents and countless countries to bring flavours from afar under one roof: your home kitchen. Every dish is accessible and fun to recreate, ranging from familiar favourites like pad Thai and katsu curry to some you may not have discovered yet — including Turkish lamb pide (savoury topped flatbreads) and Polish krokiety (filled crepes) — but are sure to tickle your tastebuds.

It should go without saying that no meal, snack or even cocktail is complete without a bit of Hendo's, so we've splashed, shaken and stirred it into every recipe. Some use it to marinate meat, others to enhance the depth of flavour in a rich sauce, and a few have even balanced the bitter with the sweet to round off your meal with dessert.

Being a celebration of culinary excellence, the book features a handpicked selection of hugely talented cooks including the twice Michelin-starred Atul Kochhar; author of the bestselling Roasting Tin cookbook series Rukmini Iyer; winner of MasterChef 2019 Irini Tzortzoglou; and champion of The Great Cookbook Challenge with Jamie Oliver, Dominique Woolf. These foodie titans rub shoulders with some of Sheffield's best restaurants, representing the array of cuisines on offer in Hendersons' home city, alongside cooks from further afield who have been enlightened with a bottle or two of Relish.

Whether you're a seasoned traveller or a home bird, this collection of unique recipes from around the world has something for everyone, and we hope you enjoy journeying through it as much as we enjoyed bringing it together. Happy cooking!

HENDO'S VS THE WORLD

CONTENTS

EUROPE

The recipes in this chapter represent a smattering of the infinite cuisines found across the continent of Europe, encompassing traditional stews from as far apart as Greece and Ireland alongside inventive twists on Polish and Puglian dishes. There's even a recipe or two to satisfy your sweet tooth; try the pears poached in Henderson's Relish and Italian brandy by Grazie or Jameson's brilliant reimagining of the tea loaf which pairs everyone's favourite table sauce with Earl Grey. Don't forget the drinks either: the master mixologists at Public have shared two of their creations for the more adventurous among us. Whatever tickles your fancy, there's plenty here to get stuck into. Enjoy!

IRINI TZORTZOGLOU

AUBERGINE, COURGETTE AND FETA BAKLAVA WITH HENDERSON'S RELISH SYRUP

PREPARATION TIME: 30-35 MINUTES // COOKING TIME: 1 HOUR 30 MINUTES // SERVES 4-6

In this recipe, a sweet-savoury syrup drizzled over the umami flavours of the aubergine, courgette and feta in the baklava takes what is already a delicious combination of ingredients to a whole new level. All you need to accompany this deeply satisfying dish is a simply dressed green leaf salad.

INGREDIENTS

For the syrup

200ml Henderson's Relish

1 tbsp thyme honey

1 cinnamon stick

3cm fresh orange peel

For the baklava

250g ricotta

200g Greek feta

2 large globe aubergines (approx. 700g)

2 large courgettes (approx. 500g)

2 tsp fine salt

100ml extra virgin olive oil (approx.)

1 banana shallot, finely chopped

3 cloves of garlic, finely chopped

60ml Henderson's Relish

Sea salt and freshly ground black pepper

25g panko breadcrumbs

1 tbsp finely chopped fresh mint

1 lemon, zested

1 x 270g packet of filo pastry (7 sheets)

To serve

Henderson's Relish syrup (see above)

A few fresh thyme leaves

2 tbsp crushed walnuts, toasted (optional)

METHOD

First, make the syrup by gently boiling the ingredients in a saucepan for about 10 minutes until thick and glossy. Leave to cool, discard the cinnamon and orange peel, then transfer to a small bowl or squeezy bottle.

Spoon the ricotta into a large bowl and crumble in the feta. Dice the aubergines and courgettes into 1cm cubes, place in separate colanders and sprinkle each with half the fine salt. Leave for 15 minutes, then rinse and squeeze out any excess moisture.

Heat a tablespoon of the oil in a large frying pan on a medium heat. Add half the aubergine and stir until soft and golden, then transfer to a bowl. Add 2 more tablespoons of oil to the pan and cook the remaining aubergine. A couple of minutes before the aubergine is cooked, add the chopped shallot and garlic and cook for a couple more minutes. Return the first batch of cooked aubergine to the pan and add the Henderson's Relish. Stir until totally evaporated. Season, stir well and leave to cool.

Cook the courgette in 2 tablespoons of oil on a high heat until golden brown, then add it to the cheeses. Stir in the panko breadcrumbs, mint, lemon zest, and freshly ground black pepper to taste.

Preheat the oven to 180°c. Spray or brush a 25cm square baking dish with olive oil, then line with a sheet of filo, allowing it to overhang. Spray with oil and top with another filo sheet in the opposite direction. Repeat with two more sheets, greasing between each one. Spread half the cooked aubergine in the dish. Spoon the cheese and courgette mix over the aubergine, smooth out and top with the remaining aubergine. Start covering the baklava with the overhanging filo sheets, spraying with the olive oil each time. Cut the remaining 3 filo sheets in half and cover the baklava, using a spatula to tuck under any excess once finished.

With a sharp knife, cut through the baklava to make 4 or 6 pieces, sprinkle with some cold water to prevent the filo from lifting as it cooks and then bake in the preheated oven for 1 hour. It should be a deep golden colour. Let the baklava stand for 5 minutes before running the knife over the original cuts. Drizzle with the Henderson's Relish syrup, then sprinkle with the thyme and walnuts if using.

GREEK

IRINI TZORTZOGLOU
BEEF STIFADO WITH SWEET ROOT VEGETABLE MASH

PREPARATION TIME: 30 MINUTES // COOKING TIME: 2 HOURS // SERVES 4

Stifado is a wonderfully rich dish, perfect for the colder winter months but delicious all year round. Henderson's Relish adds a much deeper flavour than the red wine vinegar traditionally used in the classic Greek stifado recipe.

INGREDIENTS

For the stifado

600g chuck steak cubes

4 tbsp extra virgin olive oil

1 medium onion, finely chopped

1 large cinnamon stick

2 bay leaves

5 allspice berries

75ml Henderson's Relish

250ml dry red wine

100ml passata

750ml beef stock

500g baby shallots

1 tbsp brown sugar

1 sprig of thyme

Sea salt and freshly ground black pepper

For the mash

20g unsalted butter

3 tbsp extra virgin olive oil

500g parsnips, peeled and thinly sliced

500g sweet potatoes, peeled and thinly sliced

1 sprig of thyme, plus a few extra thyme leaves

300ml vegetable stock

METHOD

Pat the cubes of beef dry on all sides. Place a sauté pan on a high heat and add 2 tablespoons of the olive oil. When the oil is smoking hot, add the beef (it's best to do this in two batches) and brown all over. Use a slotted spoon to transfer the beef to a bowl and set aside.

In the residual oil of the same pan, sweat the chopped onion with the cinnamon stick, bay leaves, and allspice berries for 3-4 minutes over a low to medium heat. Return the beef to the pan, increase the heat, and add 50ml of the Henderson's Relish. Let that almost evaporate fully and then add the red wine. Let that evaporate too and only then add the passata and beef stock. Bring to the boil, immediately lower the heat, and set your timer to cook the beef for 1 hour.

While the beef is cooking, top and tail the shallots, then blanch in boiling water for 90 seconds. Run under the cold tap to cool them before peeling. Place a clean pan on a high heat and add the remaining olive oil. Add the peeled shallots along with the sugar and sprig of thyme. Stir to brown the shallots all over, increase the heat and stir in the remaining 25ml of Henderson's Relish to glaze the shallots, then take the pan off the heat.

When the beef has been cooking for an hour, add the glazed shallots to the pan. Stir and cook for another 45-50 minutes until the sauce has thickened, adding a little boiling water during the cooking process if required. Once the meat is tender and the shallots are cooked (you want these to hold their shape) season the stifado with salt and pepper to taste, then discard the bay and cinnamon.

Meanwhile, place a clean pan on a high heat and add the butter and olive oil for the mash. Add the sliced vegetables and the sprig of thyme to the pan, stirring to coat them in the fats. Add the vegetable stock, bring to the boil, cover the pan, then lower the heat. Cook the root vegetables until tender, then use a handheld stick blender to mash the mixture. The consistency is up to you, but I think it's nice to leave some texture. Season with sea salt and freshly ground black pepper to taste.

Serve the stifado alongside the root vegetable mash, sprinkled with the fresh thyme leaves.

GREEK

MARINATED CHICKEN WITH TAHINI YOGHURT RELISH AND QUICK PITA BREADS

PREPARATION TIME: 2 HOURS 30 MINUTES // COOKING TIME: 30-35 MINUTES // SERVES 4

The chicken really improves in flavour and is more tender if marinated for at least 2 hours before cooking. You may choose to dress the pitta with finely sliced tomato and chopped onion as we would do with a souvlaki, or — as I have done here — with some shredded gem lettuce and chopped fresh parsley, simply dressed with a squeeze of lemon juice.

INGREDIENTS

For the chicken

4 chicken breasts

50ml Henderson's Relish

2 tbsp extra virgin olive oil, plus a little extra for frying

½ tsp dried oregano

1 lemon, zested

For the quick pita

320g strong (or bread) flour, plus extra for dusting

100g Greek yoghurt

2 tbsp extra virgin olive oil, plus extra for frying

1 tsp baking powder

1 tsp sea salt

½ tsp caster sugar

150ml tepid water

For the relish

100g tahini

75g Greek yoghurt

40ml Henderson's Relish

½ red chilli, deseeded and finely chopped

1 clove of garlic, finely chopped

A pinch of dried oregano

A pinch of salt and pepper

75ml water (approx.)

METHOD

Place each chicken breast between two sheets of baking parchment and flatten using a mallet, then transfer the chicken into an airtight container. Add all the remaining ingredients and massage well. Seal the container and store in the fridge. Sit at room temperature for 30 minutes before cooking.

To make the pitas, combine the flour, yoghurt, oil, baking powder, salt, and sugar. Mix with a fork a little and start adding some of the tepid water while working the dough with your hands. Go slowly towards the end and stop adding water before the dough becomes too sticky. Work the dough on a clean surface until you have a smooth ball, then place in a clean bowl dusted with flour and covered with a towel. Set the dough aside to rest for 10-15 minutes.

While the dough is resting, make the tahini and yoghurt relish. Stir all the ingredients together in a bowl, adding as little or as much water as you like depending on the consistency you prefer. Season with salt and pepper to taste.

Now place a large pan on a medium-high heat, drizzle it with a tiny amount of olive oil and cook the marinated chicken breasts for 3-4 minutes on each side. Rest for 2-3 minutes and then carve.

While the chicken is cooking, dust a clean surface with some flour. Roll out the pita dough into a sausage shape, then halve and halve again so you have 4 equal pieces. Use a rolling pin to make oblong or round pitas approximately 25cm in diameter. Add a tiny drizzle of olive oil to a pan large enough to fit the pita when laying flat and cook one at a time on a medium heat. Cook for a couple of minutes on each side until the bubbles that form are golden brown and the pita is cooked all the way through. Add a tiny amount of olive oil each time you start and turn another pita. You can make these pitas in advance and store them in the fridge wrapped in kitchen foil, in which case warm up the pitas in a preheated oven at 180°c for 10 minutes before serving them with the chicken and relish, dressing according to your preference.

GREEK

HENDERSON'S PERA

PREPARATION TIME: 30 MINUTES // COOKING TIME: 2 HOURS // SERVES 2

This delicately spiced dessert stars pears poached in Henderson's Relish and Italian brandy, served with salted caramel mascarpone and finished with grated 70% dark chocolate.

INGREDIENTS

2 medium pears

300ml Henderson's Relish

100ml Vecchia Romagna Italian brandy

100ml pear juice

85g caster sugar

1 vanilla pod

1 cinnamon stick

2-3 cardamon pods, crushed

70g mascarpone

30g salted caramel

50g 70% dark chocolate

METHOD

Peel the pears, leaving the stalk intact. Place them into a saucepan with a cup of water and the Henderson's Relish, brandy, pear juice, caster sugar, vanilla pod, cinnamon stick, and crushed cardamom pods.

Poach for 2 hours or until the pears are tender, then remove from the heat and allow to cool. Remove the pears and reduce the remaining liquid in the pan to make the sauce.

While the pears are cooling down, whisk the mascarpone and salted caramel together in a bowl until very smooth and silky, then transfer about half this mixture into a piping bag.

You're now ready to plate! Place a spoonful of salted caramel mascarpone in the centre of each plate and sit the poached pears on top. Make different sized dots of the mascarpone around the edge with the piping bag, then pour the reduced sauce into a small jug to serve alongside. Finish by grating the dark chocolate over the dessert, then serve immediately.

ITALIAN

GRAZIE

HENDERSON'S POLPO

PREPARATION TIME: 30 MINUTES // COOKING TIME: 3 HOURS // SERVES 2

This is a dish to seriously impress your dinner guests: tender octopus tentacles with a sticky Henderson's Relish glaze, nduja and potato velouté, fried Altamura bread, and stracciatella cheese. Buon appetito!

INGREDIENTS

200g octopus tentacles

Salt and pepper

2 tbsp extra virgin olive oil

2 lemons, halved

1 red chilli, chopped

A few sprigs of thyme

100ml Henderson's Relish

75ml fish stock

50g mashed potato

25g nduja

1 slice of Altamura bread

30g stracciatella cheese

Maldon salt, to taste

METHOD

Place the octopus tentacles in a large pot and cover with water. Add the salt and pepper, olive oil, halved lemons, chopped red chilli, and thyme sprigs. Bring to the boil and then simmer for about 2 hours or until the octopus is very tender. Once done, immediately transfer the octopus to a large bowl or tray of iced water; the thermostatic shock maintains the tenderness.

Meanwhile, reduce the Henderson's Relish and fish stock in a saucepan until the consistency is very thick. Blend the mashed potato with the nduja in a food processor until combined along with a little extra virgin olive oil, salt and pepper to taste. Cut out rounds of the Altamura bread with a small metal ring to create coins of bread ready for frying.

Once the octopus is cooked and chilled, place a frying pan on a medium heat. Reheat the Henderson's glaze and nduja velouté if needed. Fry the coins of bread with a little oil in the hot pan, then set aside. Fry the octopus tentacles in the same pan for 3 minutes on each side just to reheat get some colour on them, then you are ready to plate.

Dot the nduja velouté across the plate, sit the fried bread coins on top and place strands of stracciatella cheese on the coins. Place the octopus tentacles in the centre of the plate and brush with the Henderson's Relish glaze. Finish with a drizzle of extra virgin olive oil and some Maldon salt.

ITALIAN

PUBLIC

ABSOLUTELY ANYTHING

PREPARATION TIME: 24 HOURS // SERVES 1

A testament to Hendo's remarkable versatility, this zero waste coffee cocktail plays with the fruitier notes of Henderson's Relish while still showcasing its umami funk. Is it a cheeky breakfast cocktail or late-night drink that has just rolled out of bed? We'll leave that up to you.

INGREDIENTS

For the coffee vermouth
100g spent coffee grounds

500ml sweet vermouth

For the sugar syrup
250g white granulated sugar

250ml water

For the cocktail
25ml dark rum

25ml coffee vermouth

10ml amaro

5ml sugar syrup

Dash of Henderson's Relish

METHOD

For the coffee vermouth

Combine the spent coffee grounds (perfect if you've just finished your morning cafetière, or if not your local coffee shop will be more than happy to give you some from their knock-box) with the sweet vermouth in a sealed container and pop it in the fridge to infuse overnight.

The next day, pass the coffee vermouth through a coffee filter until the grounds have all been collected. Transfer the liquid into a sterilised bottle and keep refrigerated for up to 2 weeks.

For the sugar syrup

Combining the sugar and water, stir until the sugar has dissolved, then transfer to a sterilised bottle.

For the cocktail

Add all the ingredients to a mixing glass. Stir down over ice to chill and dilute, then strain into a rocks glass over ice. The garnish is up to you! We think orange or grapefruit zest works well.

COCKTAIL

PUBLIC

PIZZA ON THE ROOF

PREPARATION TIME: 24 HOURS // SERVES 1

Inspired by Breaking Bad's iconic scene in the episode 'Cabello sin Nombre', this drink takes the big flavours of the pizza that lands so gracefully on the roof and transforms them into a delicious mash up of a Dirty Martini and a Bloody Mary, garnished with crispy prosciutto.

INGREDIENTS

For the pizza water cordial

4 beef tomatoes

4 jalapeños

1 small shallot

100g fresh basil

15g fresh parsley

75ml white wine vinegar

1 tbsp salt

Granulated sugar

For the prosciutto slate

Prosciutto slices

Aleppo pepper flakes

For the cocktail

30ml bourbon

20ml dry vermouth

30ml pizza water cordial

Dash of Henderson's Relish

METHOD

For the pizza water cordial

Roughly chop the tomatoes, jalapeños, shallot, basil, and parsley. Put them all in a food processor with the vinegar and salt, then blend until smooth.

Line a sieve with cheesecloth, set it over a jug and pour the mixture into the sieve to strain. It's important to not interfere with this process as it will affect the clarity, so just whack it in the fridge and let it do its thing overnight.

The next day, it's time for straining the liquid again (yes, another one) through a coffee filter. Add granulated sugar to the double-strained liquid at a ratio of 6:1 (or to taste, depending on the sweetness of your ingredients).

Transfer the cordial into a sterilised bottle and store in the fridge. It will keep in the fridge for up to 2 weeks. Sediment may settle during this time, but you can repeat the coffee filter strain to clear this.

For the prosciutto slate

Preheat the oven to 200°c or 180°c fan. Lay the prosciutto slices evenly on a baking tray lined with parchment paper, then pop in the oven for 10 minutes or until crispy. While hot, sprinkle the prosciutto with Aleppo pepper flakes and then leave to cool. Once cool, you should be able to snap each slice in half to create your slates. Store in a sealed container in a cool and dry place.

For the cocktail

Add the bourbon, dry vermouth, pizza water cordial and Henderson's Relish into a mixing glass. Stir down to chill and dilute before straining into a Nick & Nora glass. Balance a prosciutto slate on the rim of the glass and enjoy.

COCKTAIL

MOLLY'S CAFÉ

SMOKED KIELBASA SAUSAGE ROLLS

PREPARATION TIME: 30 MINUTES // COOKING TIME: 40 MINUTES // SERVES 8

This was one of the very first dishes we created in the deli, to ease the people of Sheffield into Polish cuisine. Everyone loves a sausage roll, so we thought why not make a Polish version with the best sausage meat in the city (from EW Pearsons & Sons). It's so good we named it twice; kielbasa means sausage in Polish, so the translation is Smoked Sausage Sausage Roll!

INGREDIENTS

1 pack of ready-rolled puff pastry

1 pack of Polish smoked kielbasa
400g EW Pearsons sausage meat

Pinch of garlic salt

Pinch of pepper

Mixed herbs

1 egg

Henderson's Relish

Polish musztarda, to serve

METHOD

Roll out the ready-made puff pastry and cut directly down the middle. Slice the Polish kielbasa up and add it to the sausage meat, then season with salt, pepper, and mixed herbs.

Mix well and then form the sausage meat into two long logs. Place one log in the centre of one piece of pastry and roll it up, sealing the join with a drop of water. Repeat with the second sausage log and piece of pastry.

Separate the egg and whisk the yolk with lashings of Henderson's Relish. Cut each pastry roll into four equal pieces, making eight sausage rolls in total. Use the egg and Hendo's mixture to egg wash each sausage roll and then sprinkle with mixed herbs to finish.

Bake the sausage rolls in the oven at 180°c for 20 minutes, take out and baste again with the eggy Hendo's mixture, then bake for a further 20 minutes. Serve hot with a Polish musztarda on the side.

POLISH

MOLLY'S CAFÉ

POLISH KROKIETY

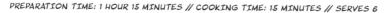

PREPARATION TIME: 1 HOUR 15 MINUTES // COOKING TIME: 15 MINUTES // SERVES 6

A staple back home, krokiety are filled crepes — here we've taken the flavour up a notch with our savoury version including wild mushrooms, sauerkraut and that all important Steel City relish. This dish flies out when we make it in the deli, especially around Christmas time as the scent of Polish ziele angielskie (allspice) fills the room.

INGREDIENTS

For the crepes

2 eggs

200g plain flour

200ml milk

100ml sparkling water

Pinch of salt

Oil for frying

For the filling

25g dried wild Polish mushrooms

100g white mushrooms, diced

1 onion, finely diced

2 cloves of garlic, finely chopped

1 jar of Polish sauerkraut

Pinch of Polish ziele angielskie (allspice)

Pinch of paprika

Pinch of pepper

Pinch of salt

Lashings of Henderson's Relish

For the coating

2 eggs, beaten

225g breadcrumbs

METHOD

First, put the dried wild mushrooms in a heatproof bowl, pour over enough boiling water to cover them and leave to soak and soften.

Meanwhile, make a pancake-like batter by whisking the eggs, flour, milk, sparkling water, and salt together. It should be slightly thinner than pancake batter to create that crepe like texture when frying.

Pour a ladle of batter into a hot non-stick pan with a little oil, fry until cooked through, then rest on kitchen paper. Repeat and once you've made a batch of 6, set them aside to cool.

Drain the soaked mushrooms and squeeze out any excess water. Slice them up, then sauté in hot oil along with the diced white mushrooms, onion, garlic, drained sauerkraut, and all the seasoning.

Add Henderson's Relish to the mushroom mixture and cook for a further 5 minutes or until reduced, then set the pan aside to cool.

Fill one of the cooled crepes with your mushroom mixture, folding gently and tucking in at each end. Repeat until all 6 are filled.

Dip each krokiety in the beaten egg, cover a plate with the breadcrumbs and roll the dipped parcels across the plate.

Fry each one until golden brown, then serve as a snack with some Polish garlic mayo or as a main meal with creamy mushroom sauce and mashed potato.

POLISH

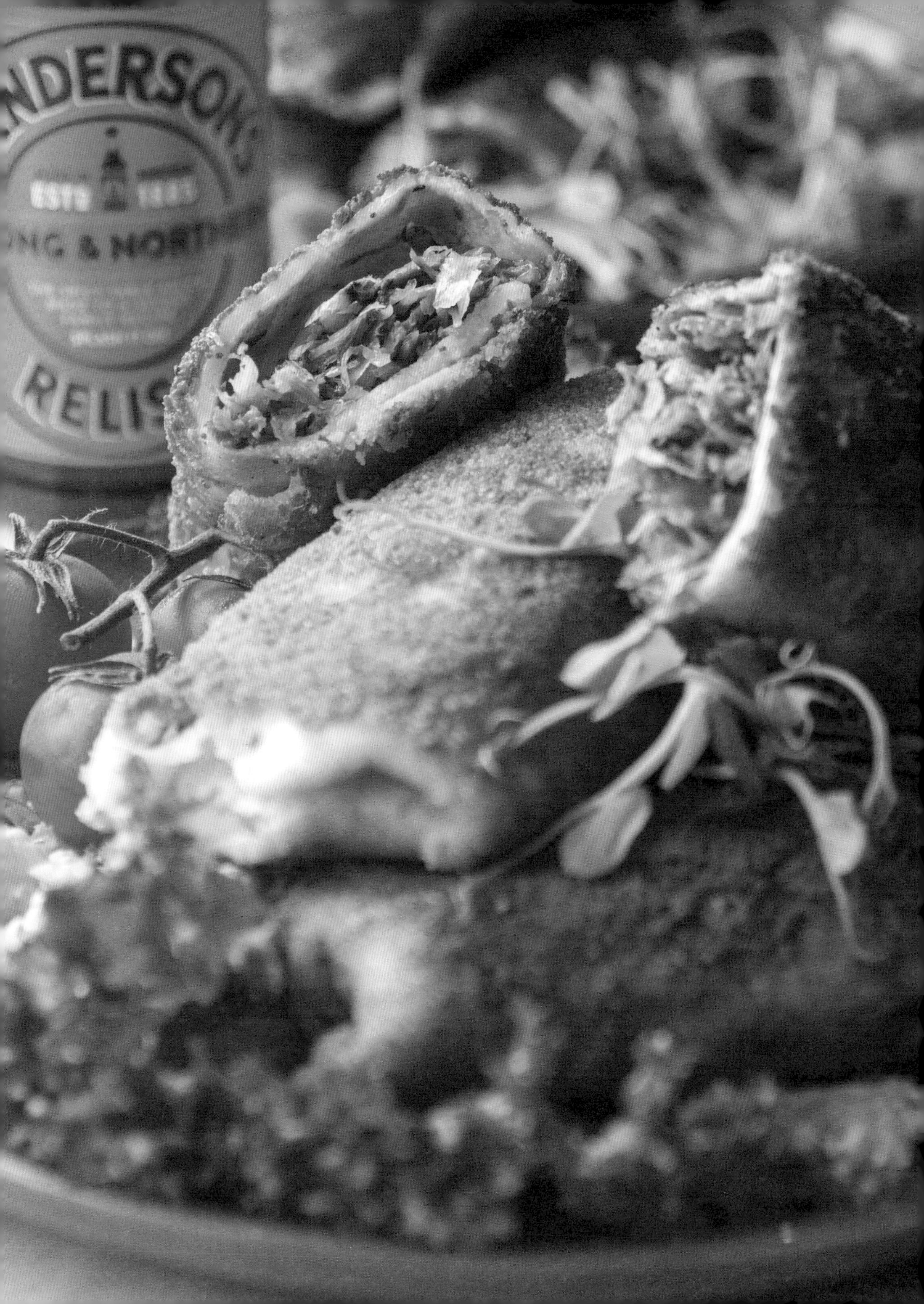

THE HENDO'S MELT

PREPARATION TIME: 5 MINUTES // COOKING TIME: 5 MINUTES // SERVES 1

This is probably one of our top sellers in the deli and a firm favourite with our regulars. It's Sheffield meets Eastern Europe — with lashings of Hendo's, grilled cheese and your choice of Polish smoked ham or streaky bacon — and easily replicated at home for a delicious breakfast, brunch or supper.

INGREDIENTS

2 slices of sourdough bread

Butter, for the bread

Lashings of Henderson's Relish

3 slices of Jarlsberg or Emmental cheese

4 slices of sopocka (Polish smoked pork loin) or bacon

Sliced onion, to taste

METHOD

Cut two slices of sourdough bread (a farmhouse granary will do but sourdough is robust enough to hold its shape) and butter one side of each slice.

On the unbuttered side of the bread, add lashings of Henderson's Relish. Layer the cheese, sopocka and sliced onion onto the relish-soaked bread.

Assemble the sandwich with the buttered sides facing outwards, then grill until you see the cheese oozing out of the sides. We serve this melt sliced in half with our homemade slaw on the side — a combination of red and white cabbage, carrot, broccoli, raisins, mayo, salad cream and seasoning.

POLISH

DOG & PARTRIDGE
BOXTY AND BANGERS WITH HENDO'S & STOUT GRAVY

PREPARATION TIME: 15 MINUTES // COOKING TIME: 30 MINUTES // SERVES 4

Boxty is a traditional Irish savoury potato pancake dating back to the 1700s. The word Boxty is an anglicisation of Arán Bocht Tí, meaning poorhouse bread. Crispy on the outside, soft and fluffy in the middle, they are easy to make and a great platform for any filling. I highly recommend a fried egg to top it off!

INGREDIENTS

For the boxty

250g cooked and mashed potato

250g raw potato, grated and washed

250g plain flour (or rice flour for gluten-free)

100g Irish cheddar cheese, grated

1 tsp baking soda

300ml buttermilk

Salt and pepper

Butter, for frying

For the filling

1 tbsp oil

450g Irish sausages (or your favourite)

1 large onion, sliced

230g mushrooms, sliced

1 clove of garlic, chopped

1 tsp thyme leaves

2 tbsp plain flour (or rice flour for gluten-free)

330ml bottled stout (not surger can)

1 tbsp Henderson's Relish

1 tbsp Dijon mustard

1 tbsp brown sugar

METHOD

First, make the batter. Mix the mashed and grated potato, plain flour, grated cheese, baking soda, and a little seasoning in a bowl. Gradually add the buttermilk while whisking until you have a thick, smooth pancake batter. Set aside.

Let's get the filling on the go. Heat the oil in a pan, add the sausages and cook until golden, about 3 minutes per side. Remove from the pan and slice.

Add the onions and mushrooms to the pan and fry until tender, about 6 minutes. Add the garlic and thyme and cook for another minute until fragrant, then sprinkle in the flour and cook for another minute. Stir in the stout, Hendo's, mustard and brown sugar, add the sliced sausage back to the pan and simmer for 10 minutes, then turn off the heat.

Pancake time… Heat a knob of butter in a clean pan on a medium heat. Add a quarter of the batter and cook for about 4 minutes on each side until golden brown. Set the first pancake aside and repeat three more times. Lay the pancakes on your plates, spoon on the filling and fold over. Top each one with a fried egg if you fancy.

IRISH

DOG & PARTRIDGE

DUBLIN CODDLE

PREPARATION TIME: 15 MINUTES // COOKING TIME: 1 HOUR, 45 MINUTES // SERVES 4

This legendary peasant stew from Dublin is simple to make, but delicious, warming and filling. This is my grandmother's recipe, enhanced with Sheffield's liquid gold. I have very fond memories of Christmas Eve when the whole family would assemble to celebrate. Everyone would bring something to eat or drink, but the centrepiece was this enormous cauldron of coddle, and of course loaves of homemade brown soda bread to mop it up.

INGREDIENTS

1 litre of water

8 thick slices of bacon, cut in strips

8 large pork sausages, cut into 2cm pieces

1kg spuds, peeled and sliced about 0.5cm thick

4 large onions, peeled and sliced

4 tbsp Henderson's Relish

4 tbsp chopped fresh parsley

Salt and pepper

METHOD

Bring the water to a boil in a large pot. Drop in the bacon and sausage, taking care not to splash yourself. Cook for 5 minutes, then fish them out and set aside. Reserve the water.

Place the meat, potatoes, onions, Hendo's and half of the parsley in a large casserole dish. Season with salt and pepper. Don't go mad with the salt though, as the bacon will increase the salty flavour. Add enough of the reserved water to just cover everything.

Place greaseproof paper on top, then cover with the lid. Simmer gently for 90 minutes until everything is cooked and soft and the liquid has reduced.

Serve the coddle in warmed bowls with the remaining parsley sprinkled on top, accompanied by brown bread and a glass of stout/tea/lemonade depending on your age and preference!

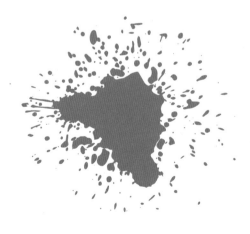

IRISH

DOG & PARTRIDGE

GARDENER'S PIE

PREPARATION TIME: 15 MINUTES // COOKING TIME: 50 MINUTES // SERVES 4-6

A take on the classic Shepherd's Pie (a staple of Irish households for generations) but meat-free. Simple, healthy and hearty, this is an ideal midweek family meal, and the Hendo's gives it a great boost. It can be prepared in advance too; rather than popping it in the oven, allow to cool in the dish, cover and refrigerate until needed, then cook for 45 minutes from chilled.

INGREDIENTS

1 tbsp olive oil

1 onion, finely chopped

1 clove of garlic, finely chopped

1 celery stalk, thinly sliced

1 red bell pepper, deseeded and finely chopped

200g white or chestnut mushrooms, thickly sliced

1 x 400g tin of chopped tomatoes

2 tbsp Henderson's Relish

1 tbsp tomato purée

1 tsp dried oregano

Salt and pepper

1 x 400g tin of kidney beans

1 x 400g tin of butter beans

2 tbsp chopped fresh parsley

900g potatoes, peeled and chopped into chunks

25g butter

1 tbsp whole milk

2 tsp wholegrain mustard

25g grated cheddar cheese

METHOD

Preheat the oven to 200°c/Gas Mark 6 unless you're making the pie in advance. Heat the oil in a large pan. Add the onion and cook gently for 3 minutes, stirring occasionally. Add the garlic, celery and red pepper and fry until just softened. Add the mushrooms and cook for 3 more minutes, stirring until lightly coloured.

Stir the chopped tomatoes, Hendo's, tomato purée, and oregano into the veg and season with salt and pepper. Bring up to the boil, then reduce the heat and simmer for 5 minutes to get the flavours combined. Add both kinds of beans and cook for 5 minutes, then stir in the parsley.

Transfer the pie filling to an ovenproof dish and set aside. Cook the spuds in a large pot of boiling salted water until tender. Drain, then mash with the butter and milk. Mix in the mustard.

Spread the mash on top of the filling in an even layer, and create texture with the tip of a fork. Sprinkle the grated cheese on top and bake for 30 minutes.

Serve at once with green veg of your choice on the side. Don't forget the bottle of Hendo's on the table for everyone to add more!

IRISH

BRATKARTOFFELN (PAN FRIED POTATOES)

PREPARATION TIME: 40 MINUTES // COOKING TIME: 10 MINUTES // SERVES 2

Bratkartoffeln literally translates to 'fried potatoes' which are usually accompanied by onions, bacon and eggs. This is a perfect breakfast dish that only takes a few minutes to cook after a little advance preparation.

INGREDIENTS

300g new potatoes

100g lardons or 4 rashers of bacon, sliced into 1cm strips

5ml oil for frying

1 small white onion, diced

15g butter

2 free-range eggs

1 tsp paprika

2 tsp Henderson's Relish

10g flat leaf parsley, roughly chopped

METHOD

Slice the new potatoes into 1cm discs and parboil in salted water until tender, then drain and leave to cool completely.

While the potatoes are cooling, start cooking the lardons gently in a frying pan with the oil so they crisp up and turn golden. Add the diced onion and cook out until sweet and translucent.

Turning up the heat, add the potatoes and butter to the bacon and onion mixture. Keep everything moving around the pan so the potatoes don't catch. Meanwhile, fry the eggs to your liking.

Once the potatoes are crisp and golden brown, finish with the paprika, Hendo's and parsley. Dish up on plates, then top with the fried eggs and another good glug of Henderson's Relish to serve.

GERMAN

CHICKEN SCHNITZEL BURGER WITH HENDERSON'S RELISH JAM

PREPARATION TIME: 30 MINUTES // COOKING TIME: 2 HOURS // SERVES 2

Chicken schnitzel is a staple dish, probably one of the first foods you think of when asked about German food. Our sweet Hendo's onion jam takes this schnitzel burger to the next level.

INGREDIENTS

For the Henderson's jam

1kg sliced red onions

400g dark brown sugar

120ml Henderson's Relish

For the chicken schnitzel

2 chicken breasts

2 eggs, beaten

50g plain flour

150g panko breadcrumbs

100ml neutral oil for frying

For the burgers

2 brioche burger buns

Mayonnaise

¼ iceberg lettuce, finely shredded

1 tomato, sliced

1-2 gherkins, sliced

METHOD

For the Henderson's jam

In a heavy-bottomed saucepan on a gentle heat, sweat the red onions until translucent, then add the dark brown sugar and Henderson's Relish. Stirring occasionally to make sure it doesn't catch and burn, reduce this down until glossy and thickened. You will know the jam is done when you run a wooden spoon through it which leaves a trail so you can see the bottom of the pan. Alternatively, you can take some out and pop it on a cold plate in the fridge to do a little set test.

For the chicken schnitzel

Butterfly the chicken breasts and flatten them out with a rolling pin. It's easier to cover them with cling film when doing this to avoid raw chicken going everywhere.

Using three large plates, set up a breadcrumbing station: one with the plain flour, one with the beaten eggs, and one with the panko breadcrumbs.

First, dip the chicken into the flour as this helps the egg stick, then into the beaten egg and finally into the panko breadcrumbs, making sure the chicken is fully coated.

In a frying pan, heat up the oil on a medium heat and fry the schnitzel until golden brown on both sides and cooked all the way through. Drain on kitchen paper to absorb the excess oil.

For the burgers

Slice the brioche buns in half and spread the bottom halves with mayonnaise. Top with the shredded lettuce, sliced tomato and gherkins, then place the chicken schnitzel on top of the salad. Add a good spoonful of the Henderson's Relish jam to the top halves of the buns and place on the schnitzel. Serve the burgers as they are or with fries if you like.

GERMAN

TWO THIRDS

HENDERSON'S RELISH CURRYWURST

PREPARATION TIME: 5 MINUTES // COOKING TIME: 15 MINUTES // SERVES 2

Currywurst is a classic German dish made from bratwurst diced up into bite-size pieces braised in beer and slathered in a curry sauce made mainly from ketchup and curry powder. We at Holy Schnitz at Two Thirds like to make it our way with the addition of Henderson's Relish and a few other bits and bobs.

INGREDIENTS

200ml vegetable stock

5 tsp mild curry powder

2 tsp smoked paprika

1 tsp onion powder

200g tomato ketchup

4 tsp Henderson's Relish

¼ tsp bicarbonate of soda

10ml oil for frying

2 large bratwursts

METHOD

For the currywurst sauce

In a large heavy-bottomed saucepan, heat the vegetable stock to a gentle simmer and then whisk in the curry powder, smoked paprika and onion powder. Allow these to 'bloom' by cooking them out and hydrating them for 2 minutes.

Next, add the tomato ketchup and Henderson's Relish, whisking thoroughly. Now carefully add the bicarbonate of soda and whisk until combined. This will make the curry sauce fizz and bubble up (hence the large pan) but don't worry, this is just neutralising some of the acid in the ketchup to make a sweeter sauce. Once the reaction is complete (when the fizzing stops), keep the sauce warm while you cook the bratwurst.

Heat the oil in a frying pan on a medium heat, then add the bratwurst and cook until golden all over. This shouldn't take longer than 10 minutes.

To serve

Slice the bratwurst into bite-size portions and cover with the warm Henderson's Relish curry sauce. This can be eaten as a snack (perfect with a German lager or two) or served with buttered new potatoes for a more substantial dish.

GERMAN

BARESCA NOTTINGHAM

HONEY & HENDO'S GLAZED CHORIZO

PREPARATION TIME: 5 MINUTES // COOKING TIME: 15 MINUTES // SERVES 3-4

This delicious tapas dish eats well with plenty of crusty bread to mop up the sticky chorizo glaze. Pair it with some aged Manchego and quince, plus sea salted padrón peppers of course, and enjoy with a crisp glass of Mahou for an unbeatable Spanish supper.

INGREDIENTS

12 mild mini cooking chorizo sausages (approx. 250g)

2 tsp olive oil

100g honey

50g Henderson's Relish

Crusty bread, to serve

METHOD

Preheat a fan oven containing a lipped roasting tray to 180°c. In a frying pan, fry the chorizo sausages in the olive oil for 2-3 minutes until they are golden brown.

Transfer the chorizo and cooking oils to the preheated tray and roast in the oven for 8-10 minutes. Once cooked through, remove from the oven. Drain off the cooking oil and reserve this for another time — it can be kept in the fridge for 3 days and is excellent for frying eggs or as a dressing.

Transfer the roasted chorizo sausages back to the dry frying pan on a low-medium heat and add the honey. Reduce this on a low-medium heat for 1-2 minutes to thicken up.

Add the Henderson's Relish to the pan and cook for a further minute. The aim is to have the glaze thick and sticky enough to coat the chorizo sausages when you pick them up.

Serve the glazed chorizo in warm serving dishes with cocktail sticks alongside some crusty bread and your choice of other tapas dishes.

SPANISH

JAMESON'S TEAROOM & KITCHENS
YORKSHIRE PLOUGHMAN'S RAREBIT WITH HENDERSON'S ONION MARMALADE

PREPARATION TIME: 20 MINUTES // COOKING TIME: 35-40 MINUTES // SERVES 2

A delicious fusion of two of our most popular classic dishes: our Yorkshire ploughman's lunch and our Henderson's rarebit. This makes the perfect lunch, brunch or afternoon light bite.

INGREDIENTS

For the onion marmalade

1 tbsp vegetable oil

2 red onions, finely sliced

4 tbsp Henderson's Relish

Pinch of dried thyme

15g sugar

For the ploughman's rarebit

Sourdough bread or crumpets

150g hand carved Yorkshire ham, chopped

50g red cheddar cheese, grated

50g mature cheddar cheese, grated

25g Wensleydale cheese, broken into small chunks

1 egg, beaten

1 tsp wholegrain mustard

Black pepper, to taste

METHOD

For the onion marmalade

Heat the oil in a frying pan, add the onions and sauté on a gentle heat until soft. Stir in the Henderson's Relish, thyme and sugar. Cook over a low heat until the mixture has caramelised, becoming sweet and sticky, then remove from the heat and leave to cool slightly.

For the ploughman's rarebit

Lightly toast chunky slices of sourdough bread or crumpets. In a bowl, combine the chopped ham and all the cheeses with the beaten egg, mustard, and black pepper.

Spread a layer of the Hendo's onion marmalade on the toast or crumpets, then top with a layer of the ham and cheese mixture, making sure it reaches right to the edges.

Place the rarebit under a medium grill to melt, then turn up the heat to glaze the top until golden and bubbling. Serve with a crisp green salad and enjoy!

ENGLISH

EARL GREY & HENDERSON'S RELISH TEA LOAF

PREPARATION TIME: 12 HOURS // COOKING TIME: 1 HOUR 30 MINUTES // MAKES 1 2LB LOAF

Jameson's twist on a classic tea loaf, incorporating our most popular tea blend, Earl Grey, and dried fruit soaked in Henderson's Relish. Can't imagine how it tastes? Trust us and try it… it's just divine!

INGREDIENTS

100g currants

250g sultanas

300ml strong, hot Earl Grey tea

4 tbsp Henderson's Relish

275g self-raising flour

225g soft light brown sugar

1 large free-range egg, beaten

Butter, for greasing, plus extra to serve

METHOD

The day before you want to make the tea loaf, put the currants and sultanas in a bowl. Pour over the hot tea and Henderson's Relish, give it a good stir, cover and then leave to soak overnight.

The next day, preheat the oven to 150°c or 130°c fan. Grease a 2lb (900g) loaf tin with butter and then line it with greaseproof paper.

Add the flour, sugar and beaten egg to the bowl of soaked fruit. Mix thoroughly (don't worry if there's a bit of liquid left in the fruit, just mix this in too) until everything is combined.

Spoon the cake mixture into the prepared tin and level out the top. Bake in the preheated oven for 1 hour 45 minutes, or until the cake has risen and the top is just firm to the touch, but check it after 1 hour 15 minutes to see how it is doing.

Leave the loaf to cool in the tin for about 10 minutes before turning out and gently removing the greaseproof paper.

To serve

Cut the tea loaf into fairly thick slices and enjoy with a nice cup of tea! It's also delicious spread with butter and topped with a slice of cheese.

ENGLISH

THE INDIAN SUBCONTINENT

The Indian Subcontinent not only stretches across its eponymous country but also spans major landmasses within Bangladesh, Bhutan, the Maldives, Nepal, Pakistan, and Sri Lanka. Three of those countries are represented here and it probably won't escape your notice that many of this chapter's recipes are from various states and regions of India. Hendo's simply lends itself so well to the balance of spice, sweetness and sourness in these cuisines, bringing out all the different notes of flavour in the sauce itself and enhancing the delicious curries, parathas, dals, and snacks that our contributors have shared. Don't skip over the irresistible Nepalese chutney and dipping sauce or the Sri Lankan stir fries though, as venturing further afield offers yet more mouth-watering delights.

RUKMINI IYER

SPICED MUSHROOM, PISTACHIO & CRANBERRY BIRYANI PIE

PREPARATION TIME: 15 MINUTES // COOKING TIME: 45 MINUTES // SERVES 4

This is a wonderful celebratory dish, where layers of spiced mushrooms, pistachios and cranberries work beautifully with the saffron-infused rice. Traditionally for a biryani, you'd cover the pot and use a strip of pastry dough to seal the edges, but I like to use filo pastry for a crispy-topped cross between a biryani and a pie.

INGREDIENTS

2 pinches of saffron threads

1 tbsp hot milk

300g basmati rice

2 tsp sea salt flakes

30g butter

5cm fresh ginger, grated

2 cloves of garlic, grated

2 tsp ground cumin

40ml Henderson's Relish

1 tbsp neutral or olive oil

150g natural yoghurt

400g chestnut mushrooms, thickly sliced

80g unsalted pistachios

80g dried cranberries

3 sheets of filo pastry

Olive oil, to brush

1 tsp nigella seeds

METHOD

Put the saffron threads in the hot milk and leave them to infuse. Meanwhile, tip the rice into a pan of boiling water and par boil for 8 minutes. Drain well and stir through half the sea salt flakes and the butter until the rice is well coated.

Meanwhile, preheat the oven to 200°c fan. Mix the ginger, garlic, cumin, Henderson's Relish, oil, yoghurt, and remaining sea salt flakes in a large bowl before stirring through the mushrooms.

In a medium-size deep ovenproof casserole dish, alternately layer up the spiced mushrooms with a scattering of pistachios and cranberries and the rice, finishing with a layer of rice. Pour over the saffron milk, then lay a doubled-up sheet of filo pastry over the rice, scrunching it carefully into the corners of the casserole dish. Tear up the remaining sheets of filo and scrunch them over the first layer of filo. Brush with the oil, scatter with the nigella seeds, and transfer to the oven to bake for 25 minutes, until the pastry is golden brown. Serve hot, with more yoghurt alongside if you wish.

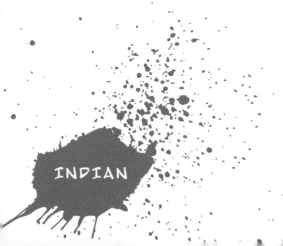

INDIAN

RUKMINI IYER
CRISPY LOADED FRIES WITH MASALA CHICKPEAS & CORIANDER CHUTNEY

PREPARATION TIME: 15 MINUTES // COOKING TIME: 1 HOUR // SERVES 4

Is there anything better than a platter of loaded fries? I think not. In this dish, crisp oven chips are topped with easy marinated chickpeas and a super-quick coriander chutney. The Henderson's Relish does the job of tamarind paste and a dozen spices, providing a brilliant depth of flavour in the chickpeas. You could use shop-bought oven fries rather than making your chips from scratch, but these are as easy and as crunchy as roast potatoes, so well worth the effort.

INGREDIENTS

1kg Maris Piper or other floury potatoes, cut into thick chips

80ml + 1 tbsp olive oil

1 tsp cumin seeds

1 onion, finely chopped

1 x 400g tin of chickpeas, drained and rinsed

120ml Henderson's Relish

120ml boiling water

50g fresh coriander, leaves and stems

10g fresh mint leaves

2.5cm fresh ginger

1 tsp sea salt

1 lime, juiced

60g natural yoghurt

100g pomegranate seeds (or ½ pomegranate, seeds only)

METHOD

Preheat the oven to 200°c fan. Tip the potato chips into a pan of boiling water, return the pan to the boil, and simmer for 5 minutes. Drain well and give the pan a little shake to rough up the edges. Put the 80ml of olive oil in your largest roasting tin (use two tins if the chips won't fit roomily in one) and pop it in the oven for 5 minutes to heat. Remove from the oven, and use tongs to gently place the chips in the hot oil, turning them evenly, making sure there's plenty of space between them. Return the tin(s) to the oven and bake for 50 minutes until the chips are golden brown and crisp.

Meanwhile, for the chickpeas, heat the remaining tablespoon of oil in a large frying pan and add the cumin seeds. Stir fry for 30 seconds on a medium heat, then add the onion and fry for 10 minutes, stirring frequently until golden brown. Add the chickpeas, Henderson's Relish, and boiling water, bring to the boil, then simmer for 10 minutes or until almost all the liquid has been absorbed or evaporated. Stir frequently to evenly coat the chickpeas in the cooking liquid. Set aside when done.

For the coriander chutney, put the coriander leaves and stems, mint, ginger, sea salt, lime juice, and half the yoghurt in a high-speed blender. Blitz, adding the remaining yoghurt as needed to loosen the mixture; you want the chutney to be the texture of single cream.

Once the chips are ready, transfer them to just one roasting tin or a serving platter, then top with the masala chickpeas, coriander chutney and pomegranate seeds. Serve immediately.

INDIAN

RUKMINI IYER
CHILLI, CHEESE & POTATO STUFFED PARATHAS

PREPARATION TIME: 50 MINUTES // COOKING TIME: 35 MINUTES // SERVES 2-3

Aloo parathas, or potato-stuffed parathas, are an Indian classic. Served alongside lime pickle and a bowl of yoghurt, they're a meal in themselves and a brilliant lunch; they'd also be lovely with scrambled eggs for brunch, or with any curry for dinner. I always add cheddar cheese to my stuffed parathas and the Henderson's Relish is a perfect way to spice up the filling.

INGREDIENTS

200g plain flour

100ml boiling water

40g natural yoghurt

1 tbsp oil

Large pinch of sea salt flakes

200g floury potatoes (such as Maris Pipers)

50g mature cheddar, grated

2 tbsp chopped fresh coriander

1 red chilli, chopped

20ml Henderson's Relish

Butter, for frying

METHOD

Mix the flour, boiling water, yoghurt, oil, and salt together in a large bowl, gently bringing everything together with a wooden spoon to form a dough. Once it's cool enough to handle, knead the dough for 5 minutes until smooth and elastic, then return it to the bowl. Cover and let it rest for 30 minutes.

Meanwhile, bring a pan of lightly salted water to the boil. Slice the potatoes into 0.5cm rounds, then simmer for 10 minutes until tender. Drain well, then mash and stir through the cheddar, coriander, chilli, and Henderson's Relish.

Divide the dough into 6 equal pieces. Keeping the remaining pieces covered, roll the first piece into a ball. Place on a lightly oiled surface, then roll out into a palm-sized circle. Put a heaped tablespoon of the potato mixture in the middle, flatten it down, then draw up three sides to form a triangle shape and pinch the edges together. Gently roll this into a larger triangle, about 3mm thick.

Heat a small dab of butter in a good non-stick frying pan. Fry the first stuffed paratha on a medium heat for 2 minutes on each side, until golden brown with a few darker patches. While it's frying, carry on rolling and filling your next paratha (or get a friend/partner to roll while you fry.) Add a dab more butter before frying the next paratha and stack the hot parathas on a plate lined with kitchen roll as you go, with another plate inverted on top to keep them hot.

Serve the stuffed parathas with yoghurt and lime pickle, or alongside any Indian meal.

INDIAN

ATUL KOCHHAR
MUMBAI LAMB SLOPPY JOES (KEEMA PAU)

PREPARATION TIME: 25-30 MINUTES // COOKING TIME: 40-45 MINUTES // SERVES 4

Here's an example of street food from Mumbai at its best. The city is the most cosmopolitan in India, and its cooking has absorbed the influences of the Parsees, the British and the Portuguese though I haven't been able to pin down exactly where keema pau came from. I loved this heavily laced with spices and butter when I was younger, but, alas, as time goes by I shy away from it, so this is my own version with less fat. Pau is the generic Hindi word for bread; you might be able to buy individual buns called paus at an Indian food shop, but otherwise soft hamburger buns are ideal. You can also replace the lamb mince with beef mince if you like.

INGREDIENTS

3cm piece of fresh ginger

4 green cardamom pods

1 black cardamom pod

2 cloves of garlic

2 red onions

2 tbsp vegetable oil

1 dried bay leaf

1 star anise

4cm cinnamon stick

300g lamb mince

2 tsp ground coriander

2 tsp ground cumin

2 tsp garam masala

½ tsp ground turmeric

8 tbsp tinned chopped tomatoes

1 tsp Henderson's Relish

Fresh coriander sprigs

½ lemon

A large knob of butter (about 15g), plus extra for buttering the buns

4 paus or soft hamburger buns, to serve

TO SERVE

1 tomato

Olive oil

Sea salt

METHOD

Remove the butter from the fridge and assemble all the ingredients and equipment before you begin. You will need 2 large non-stick sauté or frying pans. Peel and finely chop the ginger. Lightly crush the green and black cardamom pods to release the seeds. Peel and thinly slice the garlic cloves. Peel, halve and thinly slice the onions and set aside the slices from half an onion for serving.

Heat the vegetable oil over a medium-high heat in one of the sauté pans. Add the cardamom pods and seeds, the bay leaf, star anise, and cinnamon stick, and stir for 30 seconds. Add the sliced onion, sauté for 10-12 minutes until soft, then add the ginger and garlic with a pinch of salt. Sauté until the onion is softened but not coloured. Add the lamb mince to the pan, turn up the heat and stir continuously for about 5 minutes to break up the meat and brown it.

Reduce the heat to low and stir in all the ground spices. Cook for 30 seconds, watching closely so they do not burn, then stir in the tinned tomatoes and Henderson's Relish. Leave the mixture to simmer, stirring occasionally. If the mince does catch, just stir in a little water to release the crusty bits, which will add flavour (just make sure you're not stirring in any burnt bits).

Meanwhile, rinse the coriander sprigs. Set 4 aside for garnishing and chop enough leaves to make up about 2 tablespoons. Squeeze 1 tablespoon of juice from the lemon half. Stir three quarters of the chopped coriander and all the lemon juice into the lamb mixture, then add the butter and stir as it melts. Adjust the seasoning with salt, if necessary, and leave the mixture to continue simmering while you prepare the buns.

Open the paus or hamburger buns. Heat about 1 teaspoon of the olive oil in the other pan. Lightly butter the split sides of each bun. Put 1 or 2 split buns in the pan and toast on the buttered sides. Toast the remaining breads, adding a little extra oil to the pan as necessary. Thinly slice the tomato, then mix it with the reserved onion to make a salad, just like street vendors in Mumbai do.

Place the opened buns on plates and divide the lamb mixture among them. Top with the onion and tomato salad and garnish each pau with a coriander leaf.

INDIAN

ATUL KOCHHAR
GOAN FISH CURRY
(GOA PEIXE KARI)

PREPARATION TIME: 5-10 MINUTES // COOKING TIME: 30-40 MINUTES // SERVES 4

Typical of Goan curries, this is spicy with a sour tang from tamarind in the thin gravy. I love the heat; it's just a beautiful dish. Here I've pan-fried the sea bass fillets for stylish presentation, but if you want to turn this into a sharing curry to put in the centre of the table, cut the fish into bite-size pieces and gently simmer them in the gravy until the flesh flakes easily. This quantity will then serve four to six people, and all you need to complete the meal is a bowl of basmati rice. Cod and pollack are also suitable fish to use here, but they would need to simmer for just a bit longer.

INGREDIENTS

2 tbsp vegetable oil

2 medium onions, chopped

2 tbsp tinned chopped tomatoes

250ml coconut milk

200ml water

2 tbsp tamarind liquid or lemon juice

1 tsp Henderson's Relish

1 long thin green chilli

Sea salt, to taste

4 large sea bass fillets, skin on

Fresh coriander sprigs, to garnish

For the spice powder

2 large dried red chillies

1 tbsp coriander seeds

2 tsp cumin seeds

1 tsp ground turmeric

METHOD

Assemble all the ingredients and equipment before you begin. You'll need a spice grinder, 2 sauté or frying pans, one of which is large and non-stick, and a baking tray.

First, make the spice powder. Put all the ingredients in the spice grinder and grind until a fine powder forms. Set aside.

Heat the vegetable oil over a medium-high heat in the sauté pan that isn't non-stick. Add the chopped onions and cook for 12-15 minutes until light brown in colour, stirring often. Lower the heat to medium, add the spice powder, sauté for 30 seconds, then add the tomatoes and continue stirring to break down the large chunks. Watch closely so they do not burn.

Stir in the coconut milk, water, tamarind liquid, and Henderson's Relish. Slit the green chilli lengthways, then add it to the pan. Season with salt and bring the liquid to the boil, then lower the heat and leave to simmer, uncovered and stirring occasionally, while you cook the fish. You want the gravy to have a consistency like single cream.

Meanwhile, rinse a few coriander sprigs for the garnish and set aside. Pat the fish fillets dry and cut each fillet in half crossways. Use a thin knife to lightly score the skin of each fillet. Season with salt on the flesh side. Heat just enough vegetable oil to cover the surface of the non-stick pan over a medium-high heat. Add the fillets, skin side down, and fry for 3–4 minutes until the skin is browned and crisp. Gently flip the fillets over and continue frying until the flesh is opaque and cooked through. Take care not to overcook the fish.

Adjust the seasoning of the gravy with salt, if necessary, then divide it between 4 deep soup plates or bowls. Top each bowl with 2 pieces of sea bass and garnish with the coriander sprigs to serve.

INDIAN

ATUL KOCHHAR

BROCCOLI AND CASHEW CURRY (HARI GOBI AUR KAJU KARI)

PREPARATION TIME: 10-20 MINUTES // COOKING TIME: 20-30 MINUTES // SERVES 4 AS A SHARING DISH

This recipe comes from Mangalore, a lush, green part of India with large coconut, cashew nut and tamarind plantations, all of which are included in this dish along with my addition of Henderson's Relish. This is particularly good served alongside chicken and prawns.

INGREDIENTS

1 head of broccoli (about 400g)

50g unsalted raw cashew nuts

1 tbsp coconut oil

1 tsp black mustard seeds

12 fresh or dried curry leaves

Pinch of red chilli powder, or to taste

½ tsp ground coriander

¼ tsp ground turmeric

¼ tsp sea salt

2 tsp Henderson's Relish

For the coconut spice paste

1 heaped tbsp coconut oil

2 large dried red chillies

2 tsp coriander seeds

¼ tsp fenugreek seeds

4 tbsp frozen grated coconut

3 tbsp tamarind liquid

200ml water

METHOD

Bring 2 saucepans of water (one large and one small) to the boil and assemble all the ingredients before you begin. You will also need a food processor fitted with a chopping blade and a large sauté or frying pan.

Cut the broccoli into bite-size florets. Add the florets to the large pan of boiling water with half a teaspoon of salt. Bring back to the boil and cook for 2 minutes, or until the florets are tender yet still crisp. Drain well, shake dry and set aside.

Add the cashew nuts to the smaller pan, return the water to the boil and boil the cashews for 2 minutes to soften slightly. Drain well and set aside.

Meanwhile, make the coconut spice paste. Melt the coconut oil over a medium-high heat in the sauté pan. Add the dried chillies, coriander seeds and fenugreek seeds, and stir for 30 seconds until the coriander seeds crackle and the fenugreek seeds turn darker. Add the frozen coconut, then turn the heat to low and stir for 3 minutes, or until the coconut is beginning to dry. You don't want the coconut to colour, so watch closely. Stir in the tamarind liquid.

Transfer the contents of the sauté pan to the food processor, add 3 tablespoons of the water and process until the spices are finely ground. Transfer the paste to a small pan, stir in the remaining water and bring to the boil. Stir in the cashew nuts and simmer over a medium heat until required.

Wipe out the sauté pan and melt the coconut oil over a medium-high heat. Fry the mustard seeds, stirring well, until they pop. Add the blanched broccoli, curry leaves, chilli powder, ground coriander, turmeric, salt, and Henderson's Relish. Stir for 30 seconds to cook the spices. Watch closely so they do not burn.

Stir the coconut and cashew sauce into the broccoli and spices. Keep the heat high and continue stirring until the paste reduces and clings to the broccoli florets, which should be tender. Adjust the seasoning with salt if necessary and serve with your choice of accompaniments.

INDIAN

PINDY BASAN
BUTTERNUT SQUASH SABJI

PREPARATION TIME: 10 MINUTES // COOKING TIME: 40-35 MINUTES // SERVES 2

Butternut squash sabji is a North Indian dish with sweet and spicy flavours alongside a fragrant blend of spices, making it a very popular vegan dish or side. This is best served with homemade chapati or rice.

INGREDIENTS

1 butternut squash

1 red bell pepper, chopped

2 tbsp oil

2 tsp Panch Puran Five Spice (cumin, brown mustard seed, fenugreek, nigella and fennel)

1 medium onion, finely chopped

3 cloves of garlic, minced

1 tsp minced fresh ginger

1 green chilli, minced (can be deseeded for less heat, use more or less to taste)

½ tsp garam masala

½ tsp ground coriander

½ tsp mango powder

1 tsp ground turmeric

1 tsp red crushed chilli

1 tsp salt

1 tsp sugar

1 tbsp Henderson's Relish

1 fresh tomato, finely diced

2 tbsp roughly chopped coriander

METHOD

Peel the butternut squash, then deseed and chop into 2.5cm cubes. Fry the chopped red pepper in a hot pan for about 5 minutes until softened, then set aside.

Heat the oil in a wide pan and add the spice mix. Once the seeds start to crackle, add the onion and fry until translucent. Add the garlic, ginger and green chilli and fry for about 2 minutes.

Now add the garam masala, ground coriander, mango powder, turmeric, red crushed chilli, salt, and sugar. Stir well to combine and fry for about 2 minutes, then add the Henderson's Relish and chopped tomatoes. Sauté until soft before adding the chopped butternut squash.

Mix well, pour in about 60ml of water and then cover the pan with the lid. Cook the sabji on a low heat for about 5 minutes and then add the red pepper.

Cook until the butternut squash pieces are tender. Sprinkle the chopped coriander over the sabji, mix well and then turn off the heat. Serve the sabji with either homemade roti or basmati rice.

PUNJABI

PINDY BASAN
ALOO GOBI (CAULIFLOWER & POTATO SABJI)

PREPARATION TIME: 10 MINUTES // COOKING TIME: 30-35 MINUTES // SERVES 2

Aloo Gobi is a traditional vegetarian Punjabi dish served in all Punjabi households. Nutritious, simple, and full of flavour, this recipe is quick and easy to make!

INGREDIENTS

2 tbsp oil

1 tsp cumin seeds

1 medium onion, finely chopped

3 cloves of garlic, minced

1 tsp minced fresh ginger

1 green chilli, minced (can be deseeded for less heat, use more or less to taste)

½ tsp garam masala

½ tsp ground coriander

1 tsp ground turmeric

1 tsp red crushed chilli

1 tsp salt

1 tbsp Henderson's Relish

2 fresh tomatoes, finely diced

1 large cauliflower, cut into florets

400g potatoes, peeled and chopped into medium-sized chunks

2 tbsp chopped fresh coriander

METHOD

In a large frying pan, heat the oil and fry the cumin seeds until they crackle, then add the onions and fry until they turn translucent.

Stir in the garlic, ginger and green chilli, fry for about 2 minutes, then add the garam masala, ground coriander, turmeric, chilli, and salt. Stir well to combine and fry for about 2 minutes.

Now add the Henderson's Relish and chopped tomatoes, and sauté until the tomatoes are soft. Add the cauliflower and potatoes to the pan and mix well.

Pour in about 60ml of water and then cover the pan with the lid. Cook the sabji on a low flame for about 15 minutes, giving it a stir every 5 minutes.

When the vegetables are tender, sprinkle the chopped coriander over the cooked sabji, stir it through and then turn off the heat. Serve the sabji with either homemade roti or basmati rice.

PUNJABI

PINDY BASAN

TADKA DAL

PREPARATION TIME: 15 MINUTES // COOKING TIME: 30 MINUTES // SERVES 2

Tadka dal is a popular Indian dish made with red lentils and tempered in oil, with spices and herbs. This was one of my favourite childhood comfort foods and it still is now! Loaded with ginger, garlic and turmeric, it is full of medicinal properties, as well as being vegan and gluten-free.

INGREDIENTS

250g red lentils

1 tsp ground turmeric

900ml water

2 tbsp rapeseed oil

1 tsp cumin seeds

1 large onion, finely chopped

6 cloves of garlic, minced

1 tbsp minced ginger

½ tsp garam masala

½ tsp ground coriander

½ tsp crushed red chilli

1 tsp salt

2 tbsp Henderson's Relish

2 green chillies, minced (can be deseeded for less heat, use more or less to taste)

Handful of fresh coriander, to garnish

METHOD

Combine the lentils, turmeric and water in a large pot. Bring to a boil, then turn the heat down to a simmer. Skim off any foam that collects on top. Cook, partially covered, until the lentils are tender, about 20-25 minutes.

While the lentils are cooking, make the tadka. Heat a skillet over a medium heat and add the oil, cumin and onion. Temper for about 10 minutes, then add the garlic and ginger. Fry for about 4 minutes on medium heat. Add the garam masala, ground coriander, crushed red chilli, salt, Henderson's Relish, and green chilli. Stir to combine and cook for about 2 minutes.

Add the tadka to the cooked lentils, and simmer over a low heat for about 5 minutes to infuse them with flavour. If you want the dal to be thinner, just add more water and cook for another 2 minutes. Serve the tadka dal with homemade roti or basmati rice, garnished with the fresh coriander.

PUNJABI

5 TARA

NAUGHTY HENDERSON'S BHEL PURI

PREPARATION TIME: 10 MINUTES // COOKING TIME: 5 MINUTES // SERVES 4

Bhel puri is a savoury snack originally from India and is also a type of chaat. It is made of puffed rice with vegetables and a tangy tamarind sauce, and has a moreish crunchy texture.

INGREDIENTS

1 tsp oil

Pinch of salt

Pinch of ground turmeric

50g puffed rice (murmura)

50g plain besan sev

20g roasted peanuts

2 tomatoes, diced

2 onions, diced

3-4 green chillies, chopped

3-4 potatoes, boiled and cubed

1 tsp dried mango powder

1 tsp red chilli powder

1 tsp chaat masala

½ tsp rock salt

Handful of fresh coriander leaves, chopped

4 tsp tamarind chutney, or to taste

2 tsp mint chutney, or to taste

2 tsp Henderson's Relish

1 tsp lemon juice

METHOD

Heat the oil in a pan, add the salt and turmeric, stir well and then add the puffed rice. Toast this mixture on a low heat for about 3-4 minutes or until crispy. Set aside to cool.

In a mixing bowl, combine the cooled puffed rice with the besan sev, peanuts, tomatoes, onions, green chillies, and potatoes. Mix well to combine, then stir in the spices and salt.

Finally, add the fresh coriander, chutneys, Henderson's Relish, and lemon juice. Toss well to combine all the ingredients and then serve immediately, topped with some more sev and coriander leaves.

PUNJABI

5 TARA

SHEFFIELD X PUNJAB CHICKEN CURRY

PREPARATION TIME: 15 MINUTES // COOKING TIME: 30 MINUTES // SERVES 4

This spicy curry is served at the dhabas (road side diners) in North India and is full of robust flavours.

INGREDIENTS

For the marinade

750g chicken on the bone or chicken breast

100g yoghurt, beaten

1 tbsp Henderson's Relish

2-3 green chillies, slit

2 green cardamom pods

2 cloves

1 tsp red chilli powder

1 tsp ground coriander

½ tsp ground turmeric

Salt, to taste

For the curry

½ tbsp oil

1 tbsp ghee (clarified butter)

1 black cardamom pod, crushed

3-4 bay leaves

2 cloves

1 tsp cumin seeds

1 tbsp chopped ginger

6-7 cloves of garlic, crushed

5-6 medium onions, finely chopped

¼ tsp ground turmeric

1½ tsp ground coriander

1 tsp red chilli powder

2 medium tomatoes, finely chopped

Coriander sprigs, for garnish

METHOD

Combine the chicken, yoghurt, Henderson's Relish, green chillies, cardamom pods, cloves, chilli powder, ground coriander, turmeric, and salt. Mix well and set aside to marinate for 15-20 minutes.

Heat the oil and ghee in a pan, then add the black cardamom, bay leaves, cloves, and cumin seeds. Sauté until fragrant, then add the ginger and garlic. Sauté until fragrant, then add the onions and sauté until they turn brown. Stir in the turmeric and let it toast for 2 minutes, repeat with the ground coriander and then the chilli powder. Add salt to taste and mix well.

Stir in a splash of water and cook for a few minutes, then add the tomatoes. Mix well, cover and cook until the tomatoes have broken down.

Add the marinated chicken to the pan and mix well. Cook until the ghee floats on the surface of the sauce, then add water to achieve your preferred consistency. Cover the pan again and cook until the chicken is done. Garnish with the fresh coriander and serve hot with rice or roti.

PUNJABI

5 TARA

STEEL CITY MASALA PANEER TIKKA

PREPARATION TIME: 20 MINUTES // COOKING TIME: 20 MINUTES // SERVES 2

Paneer tikka is an Indian dish made from chunks of paneer — a firm, mild cheese that keeps its shape when cooked — that are marinated in spices and then grilled in a tandoor or grill pan.

INGREDIENTS

For the marinade

100g yoghurt

1 tbsp ginger garlic paste

1 tbsp Henderson's Relish

1 tbsp mustard oil

1 tsp kasuri methi

Salt to taste

1 tsp carom seeds (ajwain)

1 tbsp roasted gram flour (besan)

1 tbsp deggi mirch

¼ tsp ground turmeric

1 red bell pepper, cubed

1 bell pepper, cubed

2 onions, quartered

350g paneer, cubed

For the tikka

1 tbsp mustard oil

2 tbsp butter

1 tbsp ghee

A piece of hot charcoal

Kasuri methi, for garnish

METHOD

Combine the yoghurt, ginger garlic paste, Henderson's Relish, mustard oil, and kasuri methi in a bowl. Add the salt, carom seeds, roasted gram flour, deggi mirch, and turmeric, and mix well.

Add the prepared peppers, onions and paneer to the marinade. Mix to coat everything well, then slide the vegetables and paneer onto skewers and set aside until needed.

Heat the mustard oil to smoking point in a griddle pan, then add the butter and place the prepared paneer tikka skewers in the pan. Baste with the melted butter and turn regularly so they cook evenly on all sides.

Transfer the cooked tikka to a plate or platter with a heatproof bowl in the centre. Place the hot coal in the bowl, pour the ghee on top and cover the whole thing tightly with foil. Leave to smoke for 2 minutes, then uncover and remove the bowl. Garnish with a sprinkle of kasuri methi and serve hot with your choice of dips, sauces and chutneys.

PUNJABI

HUNGRY BUDDHA

MOMO DIPPING SAUCE

PREPARATION TIME: 10 MINUTES // COOKING TIME: 5 MINUTES // SERVES 2

The most popular street food in Nepal, momos (steamed dumplings) are hand rolled dough with meat or veg fillings. This dipping sauce is a great accompaniment for the iconic Nepalese dumplings.

INGREDIENTS

1 tbsp soy sauce

1 tbsp dark spirit vinegar (or lemon/lime juice)

½ tbsp Henderson's Relish

½ tbsp sugar

1 tbsp chilli oil*

1 tsp sesame oil

1 tbsp chopped fresh coriander

1 tbsp chopped fresh spring onion

METHOD

In a mixing bowl, whisk 2 tablespoons of water with the soy sauce, vinegar and Henderson's Relish. Add the sugar and chilli oil, mix thoroughly, then add the sesame oil, coriander and spring onion. Give the sauce a good mix to make sure everything is completely combined, then it's ready to use.

*To make your own chilli oil, combine 2 tablespoons of chilli flakes (the ones you can buy in Asian supermarkets are best) with 1 tablespoon of red chilli powder, 2 tablespoons of tomato ketchup, and a quarter teaspoon of salt. Mix well and set aside. Heat 10 tablespoons of a neutral oil (such as groundnut, rapeseed, or canola) in a small frying pan until nearly smoking, then add half a teaspoon each of minced ginger and garlic. They should barely fizz so if they sizzle and start to change colour too fast, take the pan off the heat. When fragrant, pour the hot oil into the bowl and chilli ketchup mixture well.

NEPALESE

HUNGRY BUDDHA

CARROT CHUTNEY

PREPARATION TIME: 30 MINUTES // COOKING TIME: 1 HOUR // MAKES 30 PORTIONS

This carrot chutney has always been on the menu and is much loved by our customers. The idea was to blend eastern and western taste preferences with its sweet, sour and spicy flavour profile, adding depth to our thali platter of traditional Nepalese dishes.

INGREDIENTS

300g golden caster sugar

300ml dark spirit vinegar

500g carrots, coarsely grated

80g fresh root ginger, finely grated (or 1 tablespoon ground ginger)

4 large cloves of garlic, finely chopped (or 1 tablespoon garlic powder)

50ml Henderson's Relish

1 tbsp garam masala

½ tbsp chilli powder

½ tsp sea salt

METHOD

Set a large pan over a medium heat and dissolve the sugar in a little of the vinegar, then add rest of the ingredients and bring to a simmer, stirring frequently to make sure there are no lumps from the ground spices. Reduce the heat slightly and cook on a low simmer for about 50 minutes, until the carrots are tender and starting to become translucent and the liquid has reduced. Meanwhile, sterilise your jars. Once it's ready, spoon the chutney into the warm jars, seal with lids and leave to cool before labelling and wrapping. Use within 1 month of opening.

NEPALESE

AYUBOWAN NASI GORENG

PREPARATION TIME: 10 MINUTES // COOKING TIME: 15 MINUTES // SERVES 2

Nasi Goreng is a dish that's popular on Sri Lankan street food stalls: smoky, aromatic, stir-fried basmati rice with spices, onion, garlic, chilli, and ginger, served with grilled pineapple.

INGREDIENTS

200g basmati rice

2 cloves of garlic

1 brown onion

1 carrot

1 leek

1 spring onion

150g chicken breast or green jackfruit, diced

2 pineapple rings

2 eggs

½ tbsp chilli flakes

15ml Henderson's Relish

METHOD

Ensure you have all your ingredients to hand and put the rice in a saucepan with approximately 300ml of cold water. Bring to the boil, then lower the heat and season with a pinch of salt. Pop the lid on the pan and cook for around 10 minutes. Once cooked, set aside with the lid on and leave to stand while you prepare the rest of the dish.

Peel and dice the garlic, finely chop the brown onion, peel and grate the carrot (or cut into thin strips) and slice the leek into thin rings. Finely slice the spring onion and set aside for later.

Place a wide-based frying pan on a medium heat with a little oil in. Once hot, add the diced chicken or jackfruit to the pan. Stir frequently until it starts to brown. Meanwhile, heat the grill and cook the pineapple rings until slightly browned, then set aside ready for serving.

After around 7 minutes of the chicken or jackfruit cooking, after which time it should be golden brown, add the prepared vegetables to the pan. Season with a pinch of salt and pepper.

Once the vegetables have started to soften, crack in the eggs, add the chilli flakes, and stir well. Now add the cooked rice and Henderson's Relish. Mix everything together and let it cook for 5 minutes until hot. This is your Nasi Goreng!

Serve in a rice bowl, topped with the grilled pineapple and sliced spring onion. Enjoy!

SRI LANKAN

COLUMBO

SPICY SRI LANKAN CALAMARI

PREPARATION TIME: 15 MINUTES // COOKING TIME: 7 MINUTES // SERVES 2

This zingy, spicy calamari dish is the perfect light bite to serve with drinks at your next social gathering.

INGREDIENTS

1 squid tube

2 tbsp Henderson's Relish

Pinch of black pepper

100g breadcrumbs

2 tbsp garlic powder

1 tbsp crushed dried chilli

5g fresh coriander

Vegetable oil, for frying

Plain flour, as needed

Lemon and lime wedges, to serve

METHOD

Ensure you have all your ingredients to hand and then chop the squid tube into 8 to 10 rings. Place these in a mixing bowl with the Henderson's Relish and black pepper, then leave to marinate.

In a separate bowl, combine the breadcrumbs, garlic powder and crushed chilli. Finely chop the fresh coriander and add three quarters of it to the breadcrumbs. Mix well and set aside.

Heat a good amount of vegetable oil in large pan with a wide base (the oil should cover the entire base of the pan). Meanwhile, lightly sprinkle a clean chopping board with flour, then toss the marinated squid rings in the flour until each one is lightly coated. Shake to remove the excess and then drop them into the breadcrumb mix and coat thoroughly.

Add the breaded calamari to the hot oil in the pan and fry for 7 minutes until golden brown and cooked though, turning as needed so the coating is crispy all over.

Once cooked, present the calamari in a big sharing bowl or wooden board with the wedges of lemon and lime. Sprinkle with the remaining coriander and finish with a drizzle of mayo.

SRI LANKAN

COLUMBO
SRI LANKAN CHICKEN OR JACKFRUIT DEVIL

PREPARATION TIME: 10 MINUTES // COOKING TIME: 25 MINUTES // SERVES 2

A true taste of Sri Lanka: spicy with a hint of sweetness in a sticky sauce. The chicken or jackfruit is stir-fried with onions, leeks, and peppers and cooked with garlic, ginger and chilli paste.

INGREDIENTS

150g basmati rice

15g fresh root ginger

2 cloves of garlic

1 red onion

2 large tomatoes

1 bell pepper

1 leek

1 spring onion

1 green chilli (optional)

250g chicken breast or green jackfruit, diced

2 tbsp Henderson's Relish

50ml tomato ketchup

100ml oyster sauce

1 tbsp brown sugar

METHOD

Ensure you have all your ingredients to hand and put the rice in a saucepan with approximately 300ml of cold water. Bring to the boil, then lower the heat and season with a pinch of salt. Pop the lid on the pan and cook for around 10 minutes. Once cooked, set aside with the lid on and leave to stand while you prepare the rest of the dish.

Scrape the skin off the ginger and then finely grate it. Peel and dice the garlic and onion, then dice the tomatoes, deseed the bell pepper and cut into strips, and finely chop the leek. Finely slice the spring onion and set aside for serving. If using, finely dice (and deseed if preferred) the green chilli.

Place the diced chicken or jackfruit in a mixing bowl with the Henderson's Relish, grated ginger and diced garlic. Mix well and set aside, ready to cook.

Place a wide-based frying pan on a medium heat with a little oil in. Once hot, add the marinated chicken or jackfruit to the pan. Stir frequently until it starts to brown. After around 7 minutes, at which point it should be golden brown, add the onion, tomato, pepper, and leek to the pan.

Once the vegetables have started to soften, add the chopped chilli if using (if you don't like it too spicy, just leave this out!) and then stir in the ketchup, oyster sauce, and sugar. Mix well and let this cook for 5 minutes until hot. This is your devil dish!

Fluff up the cooked rice in the pan using a fork, then serve alongside the chicken or jackfruit mixture and top with the spring onion. Enjoy your tasty Ayubowan devil dish!

SRI LANKAN

ASHOKA

HENDERSON'S SOUTH INDIAN MUSSELS

PREPARATION TIME: 15 MINUTES // COOKING TIME: 10 MINUTES // SERVES 4

We wanted to incorporate South Indian flavours into this dish as well as using seafood commonly found on the shores in that part of the country.

INGREDIENTS

1kg mussels

1 red chilli

4 cloves of garlic

2 spring onions

2 tbsp oil

1 tbsp freshly grated ginger

1 tsp brown mustard seeds

1 tsp cumin seeds

1 tsp fennel seeds

1 tsp Kashmiri red chilli powder

1 tsp ground turmeric

1 tsp garam masala

½ tsp cracked black pepper

¼ tsp salt

1½ tbsp Henderson's Relish

1 tin of coconut milk

50ml water

METHOD

First, prepare all your ingredients. Wash and clean the mussels, then finely slice the chilli, garlic and spring onion. Have everything else measured out and to hand as this is a quick recipe.

Place a kadai or wok over a high heat and when it is shimmering, add the oil. Throw in the chilli, garlic, and white parts of the spring onion along with the grated ginger, all the spices, and salt.

Stir this mixture for 30 seconds before adding the Henderson's Relish and mussels. Place a lid on the pan and cook for 3-4 minutes, occasionally giving the pan a shake.

Pour the coconut milk into the pan, stir well and cook for a further 2 minutes. Add the water if needed to loosen the sauce.

Once all the mussels have opened (discard any that remain closed) garnish the dish with the green parts of the spring onion and serve with crispy overdone naan bread for soaking up all the sauce.

INDIAN

ASHOKA

HENDERSON'S RACK OF LAMB

PREPARATION TIME: 4 HOURS // COOKING TIME: 20-30 MINUTES // SERVES 2

With this recipe we wanted to combine one of our best sellers (lamb chops) with marination, which is one of the main ways Henderson's Relish distinguishes itself from other English sauces in cooking.

INGREDIENTS

1 rack of lamb

1½ tbsp Henderson's Relish

5 cloves, toasted and crushed

1 tbsp garam masala

1 tsp ground turmeric

1 tsp ginger paste

1 tsp garlic paste

2 tbsp olive oil

4 baby aubergines

1 tin of chopped tomatoes

1 clove of garlic, minced

1 tsp ground cumin

Salt and pepper, to taste

Chopped fresh parsley, to taste

METHOD

Pat the rack of lamb dry. Combine the Henderson's Relish with the cloves, garam masala, turmeric, ginger, and garlic. Rub this mixture all over the lamb and then leave to marinate for 4 hours.

Once the lamb rack has marinated, seal it all over in a red-hot pan with half the oil. Once browned, transfer the lamb to a preheated oven at 180°c and cook until the core temperature of the meat reaches 55-60°c for medium rare.

Meanwhile, slice the baby aubergines in half lengthways, brush the cut sides with Henderson's Relish and the remaining oil, then sear in a hot pan for 3 minutes or until softened.

Make a simple sauce by combining the chopped tomatoes, garlic, cumin, salt, pepper, and parsley in a pan over a medium heat. Bring to the boil and then simmer until everything is ready to serve.

Once cooked to your liking, slice the lamb rack into chops and serve with the charred baby aubergines and tomato sauce.

INDIAN

HENDERSON'S CHANNA DAL

PREPARATION TIME: 2 HOURS, 30 MINUTES // COOKING TIME: 45 MINUTES // SERVES 2 AS A MAIN OR 4 AS A SIDE

This dish really is the best comfort food and aligns perfectly with who we are: inspired by India, made in Sheffield. The combination of earthy dal with Henderson's Relish is like the fluffiest of duvets on a cold wintery night.

INGREDIENTS

200g split chickpeas

2 tbsp olive oil

1 red onion, diced

4 cloves of garlic, minced

2 tbsp freshly grated ginger

2 tsp garam masala, or to taste

1 tin of chopped tomatoes

300ml water

4 tbsp Henderson's Relish

¼ tsp each salt and pepper, or to taste

100g cooked whole chickpeas (tinned or jarred)

Handful of fresh coriander, finely chopped (leaves and stems)

METHOD

Soak the split chickpeas in water for 2 hours or overnight, then drain well.

Heat the oil in a large pan on a medium heat and add the onion, garlic, ginger, and garam masala.

Cook this mixture for about 3-5 minutes until the onions are translucent and fragrant, then add the soaked split chickpeas, chopped tomatoes, and water.

Cover the pan and cook for 20-25 minutes, stirring occasionally. After this time, add the Henderson's Relish and cook for another 10 minutes.

Give the dal a good stir, add the salt and pepper plus more garam masala to taste, then stir in the whole chickpeas to cook for a final 5 minutes.

Add the fresh coriander, mix well and then serve the dal with your choice of basmati rice or roti. It's great with yoghurt flavoured with lemon zest on the side too.

INDIAN

TORIE TRUE

PEPPERED PORK AND PINEAPPLE

PREPARATION TIME: 10 MINUTES // COOKING TIME: 1 HOUR 10 MINUTES // SERVES 6

This pork curry is spiced and yet not spicy, unless of course you wish to add fresh chillies, which is totally optional. There are sweet notes, owing to the addition of pineapple, which work so well with the peppery spiced pork. The addition of Henderson's Relish totally elevates the curry to another level of deliciousness. A crowd pleaser for the whole family and a great curry to make ahead of time.

INGREDIENTS

3 tbsp sunflower or vegetable oil

1 tsp cumin seeds

2 x 3-inch pandan leaf pieces

20 fresh or frozen curry leaves

1 large red onion, finely chopped

1 tsp salt, to taste

6 cloves of garlic, halved

50g fresh ginger, finely grated

2 fresh green chillies, sliced lengthways (optional)

1.3kg pork shoulder, cut into bite-size cubes

1 tsp ground coriander

1 tsp ground turmeric

1 tsp ground cumin

4 tbsp Henderson's Relish

300g fresh pineapple, cut into bite-size cubes

For the masala

10 fresh or frozen curry leaves

4 whole green cardamom pods

2 whole black cardamom pods

2 x 2-inch pieces of cinnamon or cassia bark

3 cloves

1 tbsp black peppercorns

1 heaped tsp fennel seeds

METHOD

Begin by making the masala. Heat a frying pan, add all the masala ingredients and move them around the pan for 1-2 minutes, to allow the aromas from the spices to really awaken. Remove from the pan and place in a bowl to cool.

Transfer the cooled masala ingredients to a spice/coffee grinder or pestle and mortar and grind to a fine powder. Now preheat your oven to 200°c/180°c fan/400°F/Gas Mark 6.

Heat the oil in a large cast-iron pan (with a lid) on a medium heat, then add the cumin seeds, pandan leaves, curry leaves, and red onion. Move them around the pan and allow the onion to soften over the course of 6-8 minutes. Add the salt to speed up this process.

Add the garlic, grated ginger and fresh chillies (if using) to the pan. Move everything around for a minute before adding the cubed pork, folding the meat into the onion and spices.

Stir in the masala powder, ground spices, Henderson's Relish and fresh pineapple. Mix well and then simmer for 10 minutes, moving the pork around with a spoon intermittently.

Place the lid on the pan and transfer it to the oven, then leave the pork to cook for 1 hour until tender. Stir a couple of times halfway through. If it is looking very dry and catching on the bottom of the pan, simply add a splash of water to help loosen everything.

Once the pork is ready, taste it to test the salt level and add a little more if required before serving with rice or your preferred accompaniment.

Notes: Both fresh pandan and curry leaves can easily be sourced online. Keep them in the freezer and cook from frozen. Their aroma will last for months this way.

INDIAN

TORIE TRUE

CHICKPEAS WITH COCONUT, TURMERIC AND KALE

PREPARATION TIME: 10 MINUTES // COOKING TIME: 25 MINUTES // SERVES 4

This chickpea curry is so quick and easy to rustle up as the ingredients are mainly store cupboard staples. I like to use jarred chickpeas as I feel the taste is superior, but if you can only find tinned then absolutely use them. Equally I like to pop in some kale at the very end, but you can use any leafy greens you have to hand (spinach, chard, etc.). This curry is a nod to South Indian chickpea curries, due to the use of coconut milk, but I've used Henderson's Relish instead of tamarind, which adds a tasty, tangy, sweet, and lightly sour note to the dish. It can be eaten as a meal on its own or with rice.

INGREDIENTS

2 tbsp coconut oil

1 tsp cumin seeds

1 tsp fennel seeds

2 dried red chillies, broken in half (or 1 tsp chilli flakes)

1 large white onion, finely diced

1 tsp salt

5 cloves of garlic, peeled and finely grated or diced

45g fresh ginger, peeled and finely grated or diced

1 tsp ground turmeric

3 twists of black pepper

2 tbsp Henderson's Relish

700g jarred or tinned chickpeas

1 x 400g tin of full-fat coconut milk

150ml water (if you drained your chickpeas)

3 cavolo nero leaves

METHOD

First, heat the coconut oil in a large pan. I like to use my cast-iron pan, which prevents anything sticking on the bottom and, I find, really elevates all the flavours of this recipe.

Once the oil is hot, add the cumin and fennel seeds followed by the dried red chillies. After 20 seconds, add the onion and salt.

Simmer gently for 5–7 minutes, so that the onion loses its raw smell and looks translucent and lightly bronzed.

Now add the garlic and ginger to the pan, mixing them in well. After a further 3 minutes, add the ground turmeric, followed by the black pepper. The piperine in the black pepper will speed up the absorption of the curcumin in the turmeric when this dish is eaten.

Next, add the Henderson's Relish followed by the chickpeas. You can use the water that the chickpeas were in or drain them — it's up to you.

Stir in the coconut milk. If you drained the chickpeas, add the 150ml of fresh water here as well. Simmer the curry on a medium heat for 10–12 minutes.

Remove the stalks from the cavolo nero and discard. Wash the leaves, finely chop them, and add to the pan. Simmer the curry for 5 more minutes. You may find it needs a looser consistency, in which case add a little more water at this stage.

Taste the dish to check the seasoning and then serve hot.

INDIAN

TORIE TRUE

MUMBAI CHILLI CHEESE TOASTIE

PREPARATION TIME: 10 MINUTES // COOKING TIME: 10 MINUTES // SERVES 4

I have loved cheese toasties for as long as I can remember. This version takes them to a whole new level of deliciousness. It has echoes of the Mumbai variety, minus the potato, which in addition to cheese is filled with red onion, tomato, chaat masala, coriander, and mint chutney. Taking it up one notch further, the Henderson's Relish adds some fruity notes which works a treat.

INGREDIENTS

8 slices of white bread

Plenty of softened butter

2 large tomatoes, thinly sliced

1 red onion, finely sliced

Chaat masala

Cheddar cheese, grated

4 tbsp Henderson's Relish

For the green chutney

40g fresh coriander

10g fresh mint leaves

2 fresh green chillies, ends removed

25g fresh ginger, finely grated

25ml water

Juice of 1 lime

1 tsp caster sugar

¼ tsp salt

METHOD

First, make the green chutney by blitzing all the ingredients together to form a smooth sauce, the same consistency as tomato ketchup. Add more salt, sugar, and water to taste.

Take a slice of bread and slather a generous amount of butter on one side, then place in your pan or toastie maker. On the other side of the bread, slather on some of the green chutney.

Add the thinly sliced tomato and red onion, then sprinkle with a generous pinch of chaat masala. Follow this with a layer of grated cheese and a tablespoon of Henderson's Relish.

Take the next slice of bread, coat one side with green chutney and place it face down on the sandwich, then slather some butter on the outside.

If you are using a toastie maker, close the lid until both sides of the toastie are nicely bronzed. If using a pan, you may find you need a weight to press down on the toastie and help melt the cheese. You can do this by placing a side plate on the toastie with something heavy perched on top. Carefully turn the toastie over after a few minutes using a spatula.

The cheese should be oozing nicely and all the ingredients melded together, resulting in the tastiest of toasties. Repeat with the remaining ingredients, serve and enjoy!

INDIAN

EAST & SOUTHEAST ASIA

The cuisines of East and Southeast Asia are known for their incredible variety, from aromatic and soothing to sinus-clearing heat, with major influences from China to the northeast and India to the west. Of the food featured in this chapter, Thailand and Malaysia are considered southeastern while China and Japan fall under the eastern expanse of this vast continent. Cook your way through an authentic prawn pad thai, rustic Sichuan stir fried pork belly, comforting katsu curry and many more. Used to enhance dipping sauces, replicate the sweet and sour flavour of tamarind, pickle vegetables, and marinate meat, Hendo's finds its place very happily among these irresistible recipes.

FARMER'S STIR-FRIED PORK BELLY

PREPARATION TIME: 10 MINUTES // COOKING TIME: 8 MINUTES // SERVES 2

This is a traditional, home-cooked dish in the provinces of Sichuan and Hunan. It's spicy, with tender pork belly and a little hint of vinegar that whets your appetite. It is also commonly named 'small stir-fried pork' due to the dish's origins in rural areas, where it was fried in a small pot over a high flame.

INGREDIENTS

300g pork belly

1 tbsp light soy sauce

½ tsp salt

½ tsp ground white pepper

100g fresh green chillies

100g fresh red chillies

20g fresh garlic, sliced

10g fresh ginger, sliced

3g dried red chilli

50g black fungus (wood ear mushroom)

2 tbsp vegetable oil

3g Sichuan peppercorns

1 tsp black bean paste

1 spring onion, sliced

1½ tbsp Henderson's Relish

1 tbsp Shaoxing cooking wine

½ tbsp dark soy sauce

½ tsp white sugar

2g white sesame seeds, to garnish

METHOD

Cut the pork belly into thin slices, put them into a bowl and add the light soy sauce, salt, and white pepper. Leave the pork to marinate for 10 minutes while you de-stem and deseed the green and red chillies before slicing them diagonally. Get your sliced garlic and ginger ready, chop the dried red chilli and set aside. Pour boiling water over the black fungus to rehydrate it, then drain and set aside.

Heat the wok until smoking, add the vegetable oil and then put the marinated pork belly in straight away. Stir-fry over a low heat until oil comes out of the meat and the slices start to roll up slightly as they turn golden brown. Remove the pork from the wok, leaving the oil, and set aside.

Add the garlic, ginger, dried red chilli, Sichuan peppercorns, and black bean paste to the wok. Stir-fry until the aroma is released, then add the sliced fresh chillies and stir-fry over a medium heat until they soften. Add pork belly back into the wok along with the black fungus and continue to stir-fry over a high heat for 1 minute.

Finally, add the spring onion, Henderson's Relish, Shaoxing cooking wine, dark soy sauce, and white sugar to the wok. Stir-fry everything for about 30 seconds, making sure all the ingredients are mixed well. Turn off the heat, transfer the cooked pork belly to a plate and sprinkle with the white sesame seeds. For the best flavour, serve immediately.

CHINESE

YUXIANG AUBERGINE

PREPARATION TIME: 15 MINUTES // COOKING TIME: 10 MINUTES // SERVES 2

Yuxiang is a famous seasoning mixture in Chinese cuisine which originated from Sichuan province. Despite the term meaning 'fish fragrance' in Chinese, it contains no fish or seafood. Yuxiang aubergine is a symbolic Sichuan dish in Chinese cuisine which has salty, sour, sweet, spicy, fragrant, and fresh characteristics and is loaded with the holy trinity of spring onion, ginger, and garlic.

INGREDIENTS

2 aubergines

1½ tsp salt

2½ tsp cornstarch

3 tbsp vegetable oil

4 tsp minced garlic

4 tsp minced fresh ginger

2 red chillies, finely chopped

2 tbsp Sichuan chilli bean paste (doubanjiang)

3 tbsp Henderson's Relish

2 tbsp Shaoxing wine (or dry sherry)

1 tbsp white sugar

2 tsp soy sauce

4 spring onions, cut into 1cm pieces

Fresh coriander, roughly chopped

METHOD

Trim the aubergines, split them into quarters lengthwise and cut into 8-10cm lengths, then place in a big bowl. Add the salt, cover with water, then leave to soak for 15 minutes. Squeeze the water out of the aubergine with your hands, place it on a plate and sprinkle the cornstarch all over the aubergine, making sure each piece is fully coated.

Next, heat the oil in a wok until smoking. Reduce the heat to medium and add the aubergine, stir frying until the aubergine becomes softened and golden brown on all sides, which should take about 5 minutes. Remove the aubergine from the wok and put it aside.

Using the same wok over a high heat, add the minced garlic, ginger and chopped chilli. Stir until they become fragrant and any raw bite is gone. Add the chilli bean paste to the wok and stir-fry for about 30 seconds until fragrant. Put the aubergine back into the wok along with the Henderson's Relish, Shaoxing wine, white sugar, and soy sauce. Stir and toss the mixture constantly for about 3 minutes until the sauce is thick, glossy and coats the aubergine nicely.

Finally, add the spring onions to the wok, mix well and fry for 30 seconds. Turn off the heat, transfer the cooked aubergine to a serving plate, garnish with the fresh coriander and serve immediately with steamed jasmine rice.

CHINESE

CHINA RED

TIGER-SKINNED GREEN CHILLIES

PREPARATION TIME: 5 MINUTES // COOKING TIME: 8 MINUTES // SERVES 2

Also known as sweet and sour chilli peppers, this dish is named after the charred spots on the chillies as their mottled appearance resembles tiger patterns. It originated in Sichuan, but nowadays it can be seen everywhere in street food and even on family dining tables. Those who like spice can choose slim chillies, while for those who can't handle too much spice, milder large chillies are a great swap.

INGREDIENTS

300g fresh green chillies

3 tbsp Henderson's Relish

2 tbsp light soy sauce

1 tbsp white sugar

1 tsp salt

4 tbsp vegetable oil

10g fresh garlic, chopped

METHOD

Wash the fresh green chillies, then remove the stems, seeds and white parts from inside. Prepare the sauce by combining the Henderson's Relish, light soy sauce, white sugar, and salt in a bowl. Mix well and set aside.

Heat the wok until smoking, add 3 tablespoons of the vegetable oil and heat for 10 seconds, then reduce the heat to low and add the prepared green chillies to the wok. Press firmly with a spatula and turn the chillies regularly so that the skins are in even contact with the wok. Continue occasionally turning the chillies until they are soft and have a 'tiger' pattern all over, which should take about 5 minutes. Make sure you use a low heat all the time as if the heat is too high, the chillies will burn too quickly, and the beautiful patterning will not occur. Once done, remove the chillies from the wok and set aside on a plate.

Finally, return the wok to a high heat with the remaining tablespoon of oil. Once the oil is hot, add the chopped garlic and stir-fry until fragrant. Add the green chillies back to the wok, pour in the prepared sauce and cook on a high heat until the sauce thickens, which should take about 2 minutes. Turn off the heat, transfer the cooked green chillies in their sauce to a plate, and serve immediately with steamed jasmine rice.

CHINESE

GUYSHI

KUSHIYAKI - JAPANESE BEEF SKEWERS

PREPARATION TIME: 15 MINUTES, PLUS 30 MINUTES MARINATING // COOKING TIME: 10 MINUTES // SERVES 2

The savoury and slightly tangy notes of Henderson's Relish meld perfectly with charred beef, though this can also be substituted for other proteins or vegetarian/vegan options. These skewers are excellent with steamed rice or a fresh salad.

INGREDIENTS

For the marinade

2 tbsp Henderson's Relish, plus extra for glazing

1 tbsp soy sauce

1 tbsp olive oil

1 clove of garlic, minced

½ tsp grated fresh ginger

½ tsp brown sugar

Salt and black pepper, to taste

300g beef sirloin, thinly sliced into strips

For the skewers

1 red bell pepper, cut into 2.5cm pieces

1 green bell pepper, cut into 2.5cm pieces

1 red onion, cut into 2.5cm pieces

6-8 wooden skewers, soaked in water for 30 minutes

For the dip

3 tsp soy sauce

2 tsp mirin

1 tsp sake

1 tsp minced garlic

1 tsp minced ginger

1 tsp Henderson's Relish

METHOD

In a bowl, combine the Henderson's Relish, soy sauce, olive oil, minced garlic, grated ginger, brown sugar, salt, and black pepper. Mix well.

Place the thinly sliced beef strips in a sealable bag or a shallow dish. Pour the marinade over the beef, ensuring it's evenly coated. Seal the bag or cover the dish and refrigerate for at least 30 minutes, allowing the beef to marinate and absorb the flavours.

While the beef is marinating, soak the skewers, then alternate threading the marinated beef strips, bell pepper pieces, and red onion pieces onto the soaked skewers.

Preheat your grill to medium-high heat and oil the grill grates to prevent sticking. Place the skewers on the grill and cook for about 4-5 minutes per side, or until the beef is cooked to your liking and the vegetables are slightly charred and tender.

During the last few minutes of grilling, glaze the skewers with additional Henderson's Relish. Be sure to turn the skewers and baste them on both sides.

Once the beef is cooked and the skewers are nicely glazed, remove them from the grill. Combine all the ingredients for the dip in a small bowl and serve it alongside the hot beef skewers. Garnish with chopped fresh herbs if desired.

JAPANESE

GUYSHI

CHICKEN KATSU WITH RICE

PREPARATION TIME: 15 MINUTES // COOKING TIME: 15 MINUTES // SERVES 2

This delectable dish seamlessly marries Sheffield's beloved condiment with a Japanese culinary classic. This recipe also works well with pork cutlet instead of chicken (called tonkatsu).

INGREDIENTS

For the rice

200g Japanese sushi rice or medium-grain rice

360ml water

2 tbsp rice vinegar

1 tbsp sugar

½ tsp salt

For the chicken katsu

2 boneless, skinless chicken breasts (about 200g each)

2 tbsp Henderson's Relish

Salt and black pepper, to taste

100g plain flour

2 large eggs, beaten

150g panko breadcrumbs

Vegetable oil, for frying

To serve

5 tbsp Japanese mayonnaise

2 tsp Henderson's Relish

Chopped fresh parsley

Lemon wedges

METHOD

For the rice

Rinse the rice under cold water until the water runs clear. In a medium saucepan, combine the rice and water. Bring to a boil, then reduce the heat to low, cover and simmer for about 15 minutes, or until the rice is tender and the water has been absorbed.

In a small bowl, mix the rice vinegar, sugar, and salt together. While the rice is still warm, drizzle the vinegar mixture over it and gently fold in using a wooden spoon or plastic spatula. Allow the rice to cool to room temperature.

For the chicken katsu

While the rice is cooking, prepare the chicken. Place each chicken breast between two sheets of plastic wrap and gently pound them to an even thickness of about half an inch.

In a small bowl, mix the Henderson's Relish with a pinch of salt and black pepper. Brush this mixture over both sides of the chicken breasts.

Set up a breading station with three shallow bowls: one for the flour, one for the beaten eggs, and one for the panko breadcrumbs.

Dredge each chicken breast in the flour, then dip into the beaten eggs, and finally coat with panko breadcrumbs, pressing the breadcrumbs onto the chicken so the coating adheres.

Heat about an inch of vegetable oil in a large frying pan over a medium-high heat until it reaches 175°c. Carefully place the breaded chicken breasts into the hot oil and fry for about 4-5 minutes per side, or until they are golden brown and cooked through. Drain on paper towels.

To serve

Mix the mayonnaise and Henderson's Relish together. Slice the chicken katsu into strips. Divide the seasoned rice between two plates, place the chicken katsu on top, and drizzle with the Hendo's sauce or have it on the side to dip into. Garnish with chopped fresh parsley and lemon wedges.

JAPANESE

GUYSHI

ASSORTED TEMPURA

PREPARATION TIME: 20 MINUTES // COOKING TIME: 15 MINUTES // SERVES 4

Here we take the traditional Japanese technique of tempura frying and introduce it to the rich, robust flavours of Henderson's Relish. This creative cultural collision results in a crispy, mouth-watering array of tempura battered vegetables and seafood with the unmistakable tang of Hendo's.

INGREDIENTS

For the tempura batter

150g plain flour

2 tbsp cornstarch

1 tsp baking powder

A pinch of salt

1 large egg, beaten

2 tbsp Henderson's Relish

250ml ice-cold sparkling water

Ice cubes (for chilling the batter)

For the assorted tempura

Vegetable oil, for frying

A selection of vegetables and seafood, such as:

150g prawns, peeled and deveined

1 small sweet potato, thinly sliced

1 courgette, sliced into rounds

1 red bell pepper, cut into strips

1 aubergine, thinly sliced into rounds

Shiitake or button mushrooms

Broccoli florets

Green beans

For the dip

180ml dashi (Japanese soup stock)

3 tbsp soy sauce

2 tbsp mirin

2 tsp sugar

1 tsp Henderson's Relish

5cm daikon radish, grated

A pinch of sesame seeds

METHOD

Sift the plain flour, cornstarch and baking powder into a mixing bowl. Add a pinch of salt to the dry ingredients and mix well. In a separate bowl, whisk the beaten egg with the Henderson's Relish and ice-cold sparkling water.

Pour the wet ingredients into the dry ingredients and stir gently until just combined. It's okay if the batter is a bit lumpy. Half-fill a larger bowl with ice cubes and set the bowl of batter on top to keep it cold. This helps make the tempura batter crispy when cooked.

Heat the vegetable oil in a deep pan or a deep fat fryer to 180°c while you prepare the vegetables and seafood. Pat them dry with paper towels to remove excess moisture, which helps the batter adhere better.

Dip each piece of veg or seafood into the chilled tempura batter, ensuring it's fully coated. Allow any excess batter to drip off.

Carefully place the coated pieces into the hot oil, a few at a time, depending on the size of your pan or fryer. Be careful not to overcrowd the pan, as this can lower the oil temperature and make the tempura less crispy.

Fry the tempura pieces for 2-3 minutes or until they turn golden and crispy. Use a slotted spoon to remove them and drain on a plate lined with paper towels.

Mix all the ingredients for the dip together in a small bowl. Serve the hot tempura immediately alongside the dip.

JAPANESE

MAGGI GORENG

PREPARATION TIME: 15 MINUTES // COOKING TIME: 5 MINUTES // SERVES 2

Maggi Goreng is a popular street food that you can easily find anywhere in the hawker stalls of Malaysia. This stir-fried noodle dish is an all-time favourite that can be eaten any time of day for breakfast, lunch or dinner.

INGREDIENTS

2 packs of Maggi noodles

200g chicken breast

1 small carrot

1 small brown onion

1-2 spring onions

2 tbsp vegetable oil

1 tsp minced garlic

50g beansprouts

3 tbsp Henderson's Relish

1 tbsp tomato ketchup

1 tbsp paprika

1 tbsp crispy shallots

Lime wedges

METHOD

Bring a pan of water to the boil and cook the noodles for 1-2 minutes until softened, then drain and set aside. Cut the chicken breast into 2cm cubes and lightly season with salt. Peel the carrot and onion, then cut them both into thin slices. Finely chop the spring onions and set aside for garnish.

Heat the oil in a wok or frying pan on a medium heat and sauté the garlic until fragrant. Add the chicken to the pan and stir-fry for 1-2 minutes until it's about 70% cooked.

Stir in the carrot, onion, and beansprouts and fry until evenly cooked. Now add the cooked and drained noodles, Henderson's Relish, ketchup and paprika to the pan and stir fry for another 3-4 minutes. Make sure all the ingredients are thoroughly combined.

Garnish with the crispy shallots, chopped spring onion and lime wedges to serve.

MALAYSIAN

ACAR (PICKLED VEGETABLES)

PREPARATION TIME: 20 MINUTES // COOKING TIME: 20 MINUTES // SERVES 2

This Nyonya-style acar is a spicy mixed vegetable pickle, authentic to the famous dish found in Peranakan restaurants in Malaysia. It's appetising with a sour, sweet and spicy flavour, normally served as the first course of the meal or as a side dish.

INGREDIENTS

2 tbsp oil

4 tbsp sugar

½ tbsp salt

40ml distilled vinegar

60ml Henderson's Relish

5 long beans, cut into 4cm lengths

1 medium cucumber, cut into batons (skin on)

1 medium carrot, peeled and cut into batons

½ a tin of pineapple cubes, drained

For the spice paste

100g shallots, peeled

2 cloves of garlic, peeled

5g fresh turmeric root

2 macadamia nuts

1 lemongrass stalk, roughly chopped

15g dried chillies, deseeded and soaked in hot water

10g shrimp paste

METHOD

Blend all the ingredients for the spice paste with 100ml of water until smooth.

Heat the oil in a pan and add the spice paste. Sauté for 10-15 minutes until it smells aromatic and the chilli oil has separated.

Stir the sugar, salt, vinegar, and Henderson's Relish into the paste. Mix thoroughly until all the seasoning has fully dissolved, then sauté for another 5 minutes.

Take the pan off the heat and let the mixture cool down before adding all the veg and pineapple. Stir well and then transfer to an airtight container.

Leave the pickle in the fridge overnight to develop in flavour. Garnish with crispy shallots and sesame seeds to serve.

MALAYSIAN

DOMINIQUE WOOLF
THAI PORK SKEWERS WITH STICKY DIPPING SAUCE

PREPARATION TIME: 20 MINUTES, PLUS 1 HOUR FOR MARINATING // COOKING TIME: 15 MINUTES // MAKES 16 SKEWERS

A highlight of any Thai street food market has to be the charcoal-grilled pork skewers, known as moo ping: smoky, charred, aromatic, and completely irresistible! I could eat them all day long. Here I've made them with a sticky, sweet and salty dipping sauce. A match made in heaven! Any leftover sauce can be drizzled over noodles or rice dishes.

INGREDIENTS

For the pork

4 cloves of garlic, crushed

Large handful of coriander stalks, finely chopped

4 tbsp coconut milk, plus 2 tbsp for basting

2 tbsp Henderson's Relish

2 tbsp oyster sauce

1 tbsp fish sauce

1 tbsp soft brown sugar

1 tbsp cornflour

1 tbsp neutral oil (such as sunflower or rapeseed)

600g pork shoulder steaks, cut into 2.5–3cm cubes

16 bamboo skewers

For the dipping sauce

5 tbsp water

3 tbsp soft brown sugar

2 tbsp Henderson's Relish

2 tbsp fish sauce

1 tbsp honey

1 tsp chilli flakes

METHOD

Combine all the ingredients for the pork, apart from the pork itself, in a large dish. Add the pork and coat well. Cover and place in the fridge to marinate for at least 1 hour or overnight if you have time. Meanwhile, soak the bamboo skewers in water.

To make the dipping sauce, place all the ingredients into a small saucepan over a medium heat. Bring to a simmer and bubble for 5–7 minutes until it becomes slightly syrupy (it should coat the back of a metal spoon). Set aside to cool.

Thread the pork onto the skewers. Heat a griddle pan, frying pan or grill to high. You can also cook these on the barbecue. Cook the pork for 2–3 minutes on each side or until done, basting with the remaining coconut milk halfway through.

Serve the skewers immediately with the dipping sauce.

THAI

DOMINIQUE WOOLF

PRAWN PAD THAI

PREPARATION TIME: 10 MINUTES // COOKING TIME: 10 MINUTES // SERVES 2

Pad Thai was my Auntie Dang's speciality and one of my favourite dishes growing up. I still love it to this day and make it near-weekly. In this non-traditional version, I use Henderson's Relish instead of tamarind paste to create the sweet and tangy sauce; it works perfectly! This is such a tasty, moreish plate of food.

INGREDIENTS

150g flat rice noodles

1–2 tbsp neutral oil (such as sunflower or rapeseed)

2 cloves of garlic, finely chopped

3 spring onions, halved lengthways, then cut into 4cm pieces

1 carrot, cut into thin matchsticks

200g king prawns, shelled and deveined

2 eggs, lightly beaten

100g beansprouts

For the sauce

2½ tbsp soft brown sugar

2 tbsp Henderson's Relish

2 tbsp fish sauce

1 tbsp ketchup

1 tsp chilli flakes

To serve

Large handful of salted peanuts, roughly chopped

Wedges of lime

Chilli flakes

METHOD

Cook the rice noodles according to the packet instructions, being careful not to overcook them (as this will make the dish soggy). Rinse, drain and set near the stove.

Place the ingredients for the sauce in a small saucepan over a medium heat and bring to a simmer, stirring to dissolve the sugar. Turn off the heat and set aside.

Heat 1 tablespoon of the oil in a large non-stick frying pan or wok over a high heat. Once hot, add the garlic and stir-fry for around 30 seconds, being careful not to burn it. Add the white parts of the spring onion (reserving the greens) and the carrots to the pan, then stir-fry for 1 minute.

Add the prawns and stir-fry until they start to change colour (but are not yet fully cooked). Push to the back of the pan and drizzle in a little more oil. Pour in the eggs and leave to set for a few moments, then scramble until just set.

Tip in the cooked noodles and pad Thai sauce, stirring to combine everything thoroughly. Mix in the reserved spring onion greens and beansprouts, then turn off the heat.

Serve immediately with the chopped peanuts, wedges of lime and chilli flakes on top or on the side.

THAI

DOMINIQUE WOOLF

THAI BEEF SALAD

PREPARATION TIME: 15 MINUTES // COOKING TIME: 5 MINUTES // SERVES 2

This classic Thai dish has everything you would expect from a Thai salad and more: seared steak combined with peppery radishes, crunchy cucumber, juicy tomatoes and aromatic herbs, all brought together with a punchy, sweet, spicy, and tangy dressing. Absolutely delicious! It takes just minutes to make; start by marinating the steak before preparing the salad ingredients to maximise your time.

INGREDIENTS

For the steak

2 tsp Henderson's Relish

250g sirloin steak

Sea salt flakes

Black pepper

Neutral oil (such as sunflower or rapeseed)

For the salad

5 radishes, thinly sliced

6 cherry tomatoes, halved

¼ small red onion, thinly sliced

¼ cucumber, quartered lengthways and sliced

Handful of mint leaves, finely shredded

Handful of coriander leaves

50g mixed leaves

For the dressing

3 tbsp lime juice (approx. 2 limes)

1½ tbsp fish sauce

1½ tbsp soft brown sugar

1 tbsp Henderson's Relish

1 bird's eye chilli, finely chopped (deseed or use a mild red chilli if preferred)

To serve

2 tbsp salted peanuts, roughly chopped

METHOD

First, marinate the steak. Place the Henderson's Relish in a dish and add the steak, coating on both sides. Leave to marinate while you prepare the salad ingredients.

Heat a frying pan or griddle over a high heat until very hot. Drizzle a little oil on the steak and season generously with salt and pepper. Cook for 1-2 minutes on each side for rare or a minute more on each side for medium-rare, depending on the thickness of the steak. Leave to rest for 5 minutes, then thinly slice.

While the beef is resting, combine the ingredients for the dressing and stir until the sugar dissolves.

Place the salad ingredients in a large mixing bowl and add the beef, along with any juices. Pour over the dressing and gently combine.

Place on a serving dish and scatter over the peanuts. Serve immediately.

THAI

118

THE AMERICAS

Encompassing two continents, this huge geographical area can also be roughly divided into two major cultural regions: Latin America and Anglo-America. From the former, the tapas queens at La Mama have shared a few of their favourite recipes and Jamaican-born musician Franz Von puts a Hendo's twist on traditional brown stew chicken. Over in the States, get ready to indulge with glazed wings and ribs, meatloaf, burgers, onions rings and a Louisiana-style po' boy. Moving down to Mexico, we find both meat and mushroom fillings for the classic street food taco, plus Mexico's answer to a Bloody Mary. Needless to say, Henderson's Relish enhances them all so get ready to shake it in and splash it on through our whirlwind tour of the Americas.

STREET FOOD CHEF
CHIPOTLE AND HENDO'S PULLED BEEF BRISKET

PREPARATION TIME: 10 MINUTES // COOKING TIME: 4-12 HOURS // SERVES 10

This punchy beef brisket is cooked low and slow until it's so tender that the meat can be pulled apart with forks. Henderson's Relish is a vibrant and tangy condiment that adds a burst of flavour, complemented by the rich, smoky chipotle to create a delicious and satisfying dish.

INGREDIENTS

1kg beef brisket

25ml Henderson's Relish

150ml chipotles in adobo sauce

1 tsp salt

1 tsp black pepper

1 onion

METHOD

Place the brisket in a large baking tray with deep sides. Rub the meat all over with the Henderson's Relish and chipotles in adobo, then sprinkle evenly with the salt and pepper.

Cut the onion in half and place cut side down on top of the brisket. Cover the tray with foil and seal the edges tightly.

Place the brisket in the oven to cook for either about 4 hours at 175°c or about 12 hours at 110°c. The exact timing will depend on your oven, so check whether the brisket is cooked by seeing if the juices run clear and the meat falls apart easily. If it isn't ready, replace the foil and place back in the oven at a higher temperature for another 30 minutes, then check again and repeat as needed.

Once the brisket is done, leave all the juices and fat in the tray as this is the birria (sauce) and let it sit at room temperature for 45 minutes.

Pull the meat apart once rested, discarding any fatty parts, and mix it with the birria in the tray. Serve with your favourite Mexican dishes — it's the perfect filling for tacos or burritos, topped with salsa, pico de gallo, guacamole, and of course wedges of lime for squeezing over.

MEXICAN

BEEF BIRRIA TACO AND CONSOMMÉ

PREPARATION TIME: 1 HOUR // COOKING TIME: 4 HOURS 30 MINUTES // SERVES 10-15

An absolute classic, this Mexican street food taco features slow cooked, marinated beef loaded into a tortilla with melted cheese and a zingy garnish: understandably a customer favourite. We recommend using 100% corn tortillas if you can get them, but regular tortillas work fine too!

INGREDIENTS

For the beef birria

1 beef shin (approx. 2.5kg)

250ml red wine

2 white onions

2 tomatoes

1 carrot

1 stick of celery

3 fresh jalapeños

8 cloves of garlic

8 sprigs of thyme

2 sprigs of rosemary

2 sprigs of oregano

1 litre beef stock

500ml chicken stock

500ml strong real ale

300g birria marinade (our secret house blend)

150g beef dripping

50ml Henderson's Relish

3 tbsp tomato purée

For the salsa

2 ripe tomatoes

1 small red onion

1 fresh jalapeño

1 clove of garlic

To serve

Tortillas

Grated mozzarella

METHOD

For the beef birria

Preheat your oven to 160°c. Cut the beef shin into 5cm cubes, removing any tough sinew and excess fat. Coat the beef in oil and salt, then seal in a hot pan on all sides. Deglaze the pan with a splash of the red wine, then pour this and all the beef into a large ovenproof dish.

Peel and roughly chop the onions, tomatoes, carrot, celery, and jalapeños. Add these and all the remaining ingredients to the ovenproof dish and season generously with salt and pepper. Cover the surface with a piece of baking parchment and then tightly cover the dish with tin foil.

Braise the birria in the preheated oven for 3.5-4 hours until the meat falls apart. Leave to cool for 30 minutes, then use a slotted spoon to transfer the beef into a separate bowl. Pull the beef apart, removing any fatty or tough bits as you go. Pass the remaining liquid (consommé) into a tub through a sieve and discard the veg. Reheat the meat and consommé separately when you're ready to serve.

For the salsa

Quarter and deseed the tomatoes, then dice into small cubes. Dice the onion to a similar size. Deseed and finely dice the jalapeño, grate the garlic, then mix all the ingredients together in a bowl with a good pinch of salt and pepper. Leave the flavours to infuse for 30 minutes or until needed.

To serve

Place a frying pan on a medium heat. Dip your tortilla into the consommé and fry in the pan for 15-20 seconds on each side. While still in the pan, top the tortilla with grated mozzarella and leave to slowly melt. Transfer to a plate and top with a heathy portion of beef. Garnish with your pico de gallo salsa, some fresh coriander and a hot sauce of your choice (or Henderson's Relish!). Serve with a side of warmed consommé and a fat wedge of lime. Dip your taco in the consommé before eating!

MEXICAN

PIÑA

MUSHROOM ASADA TACOS

PREPARATION TIME: 30 MINUTES // COOKING TIME: 45 MINUTES // SERVES 3-4

A delicious roasted mushroom recipe. Balance the deep, rich flavour with your favourite salsa or sauce. We advise using 100% corn tortillas if you can get them, but regular tortillas work fine too!

INGREDIENTS

6 Portobello or flat cap mushrooms
25ml Henderson's Relish
10g chipotle in adobo
Juice of ½ an orange
Juice of ½ a lemon
10g fresh coriander
2 cloves of garlic
1 fresh jalapeño
½ small white onion
2 tsp ground cumin
2 tsp smoked paprika
10ml oil

To serve

Tortillas
Sauce or dip of your choice
1 white onion, finely diced
Handful of chopped coriander
1 lime, cut into wedges

METHOD

Cut the mushrooms into 5mm thick slices and put them in a large baking tray or roasting tin. Add all the remaining ingredients to a blender and blend until a paste forms.

Add the paste and a pinch of salt to the mushrooms, then leave to marinate for 30 minutes. Cook in the preheated oven for 15 minutes, stir and then return to the oven for another 15 minutes.

To serve

Warm your tortillas using a frying pan on a medium heat. Reheat the cooked mushrooms in a pan if needed and loaded onto the warmed tortillas.

Add the sauce or dip of your choice to the tacos — guacamole, salsa verde or hot sauce work well. Top each one with some finely diced white onion, fresh coriander and a squeeze of lime juice. Enjoy!

MEXICAN

PIÑA

MICHELADA

PREPARATION TIME: 5 MINUTES // SERVES 1

This is Mexico's answer to the Bloody Mary and a staff favourite! Spicy, tangy and super moreish. If you can get hold of it, clamato juice can be a great addition for a more authentic, coastal vibe.

INGREDIENTS

1 lime, halved

Tajin Lime Chilli Salt or flaky sea salt (such as Maldon)

15-25ml Mexican hot sauce (such as Valentina or Cholula)

5-6 dashes of Henderson's Relish

50ml clamato juice or tomato juice, as preferred

Mexican beer (such as Modelo or Pacifico)

Ice

METHOD

Run a wedge of lime round the rim of your glass (ideally something 16oz or above) and then dip the glass in your choice of chilli or flaky salt. This is most easily done by pouring the salt onto a small plate and gently dipping the wet rim of the glass in, bit by bit.

Juice the other half of the lime and pour this into your glass along with the hot sauce, Henderson's Relish and clamato or tomato juice. Add a small amount of beer and mix thoroughly.

Top up the glass with ice and stir gently as you add the remaining beer. Garnish as you would a Bloody Mary, anything goes!

To make multiple drinks, you can prepare a batch of the hot sauce, lime juice, Henderson's Relish and clamato juice mixture.

MEXICAN

UNIT

SHRIMP PO' BOY

PREPARATION TIME: 5-10 MINUTES // COOKING TIME: 10-15 MINUTES // SERVES 2-4

A po' boy is a hot sandwich originating from Louisiana, which usually contains roast meat or deep-fried seafood as we've gone for here — try this recipe with oysters, fish or chicken for different options too. The lightly spiced coating for the shrimp is complimented by the spicy notes of the Henderson's Relish, all wrapped up in soft rolls for a Southern classic with a British twist.

INGREDIENTS

300g shrimp, peeled and deveined

150g cornmeal or breadcrumbs

1 tsp paprika

½ tsp garlic powder

½ tsp onion powder

¼ tsp cayenne pepper (or to taste)

Salt and black pepper, to taste

Vegetable oil, for frying

2 baguettes or sub rolls

A good splash of Henderson's Relish

1 lettuce, leaves separated

1 large tomato, sliced

Pickles of your choice

METHOD

First, prepare the shrimp. In a bowl, combine the cornmeal (or breadcrumbs) with the paprika, garlic powder, onion powder, cayenne pepper, salt, and black pepper.

Dredge the shrimp in the seasoned cornmeal, pressing gently to adhere the coating. Shake off any excess.

Heat enough vegetable oil to fully submerge the shrimp in a skillet or deep fat fryer to 175°c. Carefully place the coated shrimp into the hot oil and fry for about 2-3 minutes, or until they are golden brown and crispy. Use a slotted spoon to transfer the cooked shrimp to a plate lined with paper towels to drain any excess oil.

Cut the baguettes or sub rolls in half horizontally, leaving one side attached (like a hinge). Shake a generous amount of Henderson's Relish over both sides of each one, the layer the lettuce leaves, tomato slices, and pickles on the bottom halves. Feel free to add additional toppings or sauces according to your preferences.

Arrange the fried shrimp in an even layer on top of the salad, then close the po' boys by folding the top half of the baguettes or rolls over the filling. Serve immediately while the shrimp are still warm and crispy. Enjoy!

USA

FALAFEL BURGERS

PREPARATION TIME: 15-20 MINUTES // COOKING TIME: 10-25 MINUTES // SERVES 4

These burgers have such a great combination of flavours and textures. Feel free to customise them with your favourite toppings — cheese, onions, pickles, or slices of avocado — in addition to the non-negotiable Henderson's Relish!

INGREDIENTS

2 x 400g tins of chickpeas, drained and rinsed

1 small onion, roughly chopped

3 cloves of garlic, minced

25g fresh parsley, chopped

1 tsp ground cumin

1 tsp ground coriander

½ tsp salt

¼ tsp black pepper

¼ tsp cayenne pepper (or to taste)

1 tbsp lemon juice

3-4 tbsp plain flour

Vegetable oil, for frying

A good splash of Henderson's Relish

4 burger buns

1-2 large tomatoes, sliced

1 lettuce, leaves separated

METHOD

First, prepare the falafel mixture. In a food processor, combine the chickpeas, onion, garlic, parsley, ground cumin, ground coriander, salt, black pepper, cayenne pepper, and lemon juice. Pulse until the mixture is well combined but still slightly chunky.

Transfer the mixture to a bowl and add 3 tablespoons of plain flour. Mix until the mixture holds together when pressed. If needed, add an additional tablespoon of flour to achieve the right consistency. Divide the mixture into quarters and shape each portion into a patty. You can use your hands or a burger press to do this.

Heat about half a centimetre of vegetable oil in a skillet over a medium-high heat. Carefully place the falafel patties into the hot oil and fry for about 3-4 minutes on each side, or until they are golden brown and crispy. Use a slotted spoon to transfer the cooked patties to a plate lined with paper towels to drain any excess oil.

You can also bake the falafel patties in the oven if you prefer a healthier option. For this cooking method, preheat the oven to 190°c and brush the patties with a little oil, then bake for about 20-25 minutes on a non-stick tray, flipping them over halfway through.

Toast the burger buns lightly if desired. Place a couple of lettuce leaves and tomato slices on the bottom half of each bun, then top with a falafel patty and splash generously with Henderson's Relish. Add any additional burger toppings of your choice, top with the other half of the burger bun and serve the falafel burgers immediately while they are still warm. Enjoy!

USA

CRISPY ONION RINGS WITH HENDO'S DIP

PREPARATION TIME: 5-10 MINUTES // COOKING TIME: 10-15 MINUTES // SERVES 4

What could be better than crispy, salty, freshly fried onion rings? Those onion rings dipped in Henderson's Relish, of course! The only tricky thing about this delicious recipe is the deep frying — always work carefully around hot oil, never leave it unattended, keep a fire extinguisher handy, and dispose of used oil responsibly.

INGREDIENTS

2 large white onions

400ml water

500ml sparkling water

1 tbsp baking powder

280g plain flour (approx.)

1 tbsp salt

1 tbsp black pepper

1 tbsp paprika

1 tbsp mixed herbs

50ml lemon juice

Vegetable oil, for frying

Henderson's Relish, for dipping

METHOD

Peel the onions and slice them into rings about half an inch thick. Separate the rings and set them aside while you make the batter.

In a large mixing bowl, combine the sparkling and regular water. Add the baking powder and stir until it has dissolved, then gradually add the plain flour while stirring continuously to form a smooth batter. Adjust the amount of plain flour as needed to achieve the desired consistency of the batter. It should be thick enough to coat the onion rings but not so thick that it becomes gloopy. Add the salt, pepper, paprika, mixed herbs, and lemon juice. Mix well until all the ingredients are incorporated.

Fill a deep pot or a deep fat fryer with vegetable oil and heat to 175°c. Dip each onion ring into the batter, making sure they are fully coated and allowing any excess batter to drip off.

Carefully lower the battered onion rings into the hot oil using tongs or a slotted spoon. Avoid overcrowding the pot or fryer as this can lower the oil temperature and make the rings greasy. Fry them in batches for about 2-3 minutes, or until they turn golden brown and crispy. Adjust the cooking time as needed depending on the thickness of the rings.

Once the onion rings are fried to a golden colour, use a slotted spoon to remove them from the oil and place them on a plate lined with paper towel to drain any excess oil. Sprinkle with a pinch of salt while they're still hot, then serve alongside a bowl of Henderson's Relish for dipping. Enjoy your homemade crispy onion rings as a delicious starter or snack!

USA

HENDERSON'S GLAZED BABY BACK RIBS

PREPARATION TIME: 10 MINUTES // COOKING TIME: 3 HOURS 30 MINUTES // SERVES 4

These baby back ribs will take you straight to the deep south of America. Succulent and sticky, they are guaranteed to be a hit at anything from family get-togethers to Super Bowl parties!

INGREDIENTS

2 racks of baby back ribs

120ml Henderson's Relish

60g brown sugar

30ml soy sauce

1 spring onion

20g crispy onions

Salt and pepper, to taste

METHOD

Preheat your oven to 150°c. Prepare the ribs by carefully peeling away the membrane from the back using a knife and some kitchen roll, then season generously with salt and pepper.

In a bowl, combine the Henderson's Relish, brown sugar and soy sauce. Whisk until smooth and well mixed, then brush the glaze generously over both sides of the ribs, saving about a quarter for later.

Wrap the ribs tightly in tin foil and place them on a baking tray, then place the baking tray into the preheated oven and cook for 2.5-3 hours until the ribs are tender.

Once tender, remove the foil and brush the ribs with the remaining glaze. Increase the oven temperature to 200°c and place the ribs back in the oven to cook uncovered for 15-20 minutes, until the glaze has caramelised and turned sticky.

Remove from the oven and let the ribs rest for 5 minutes, then slice between each bone. Finely slice the spring onion and sprinkle it over the ribs along with the crispy onions for some great texture.

USA

HENDERSON'S GLAZED WINGS

PREPARATION TIME: 35 MINUTES // COOKING TIME: 30 MINUTES // SERVES 2

Perfect for any occasion, these wings are guaranteed to be crispy and sticky! Serve with a ranch sauce or a blue cheese dip and celery sticks for the authentic game day experience.

INGREDIENTS

120ml Henderson's Relish

60ml honey

30ml melted butter

12 chicken wings

Salt and pepper

1 tsp chilli flakes (optional)

1 tsp sesame seeds

1 spring onion, sliced

METHOD

In a bowl, mix the Henderson's Relish, honey and melted butter until well combined. Season the chicken wings with salt, then leave to rest in the fridge for 15 minutes.

Remove the wings from the fridge and coat them in half the Hendo's glaze. Cover the bowl and leave in the fridge for another 15 minutes. Preheat your oven to 200°c.

Line a baking tray with baking parchment and place the wings on the tray, ensuring they aren't touching each other.

Place in the oven and cook for 25 minutes, turning the wings over halfway through. The wings will be done when they turn golden brown, and the internal temperature reaches 75°c.

Once out the oven, toss the wings in the remaining glaze and the chilli flakes if you want some extra heat! Sprinkle over the sesame seeds and sliced spring onion to serve.

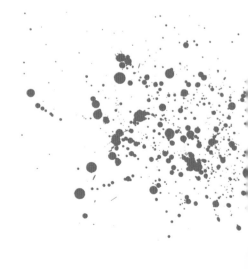

USA

SHOOT THE BULL

HENDERSON'S MEATLOAF

PREPARATION TIME: 15 MINUTES // COOKING TIME: 1 HOUR // SERVES 4

This family favourite is straight out of middle America's home kitchens. Just like mama used to make, this recipe is perfect for a midweek tea or to use up any leftover veggies from a Sunday roast!

INGREDIENTS

500g beef mince

125g breadcrumbs

60ml Henderson's Relish

60ml tomato ketchup

1 egg

Salt and pepper

METHOD

Preheat the oven to 180°c. In a large mixing bowl, combine the beef mince, breadcrumbs, Henderson's Relish, ketchup and egg. Season the mixture with salt and pepper, then using your hands to mix everything together until well combined.

Press the mixture gently into a non-stick loaf tin, moulding it into shape, then place the tin in the preheated oven and bake for 45-50 minutes until the internal temperature of the meatloaf reaches 75°c.

Once cooked, remove the meatloaf from the tin and leave it to rest for 5 minutes before slicing. Serve with mashed potato, roast vegetables and gravy for the authentic American meal.

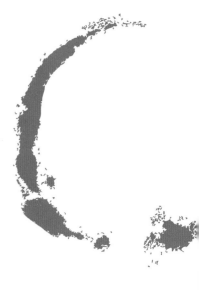

USA

CHILEAN BEEF EMPANADAS

PREPARATION TIME: 1 HOUR // COOKING TIME: 30 MINUTES // MAKES 8-10

Many families have these empanadas de pino for lunch every Sunday in Chile. I remember making them in England with my grandmother (mami) and granddad (tata) on a Sunday, with the Eastenders omnibus in the background! First, you make the pino filling — a mapuche name meaning spiced beef and onions — and then the dough. It was, and still is, a great way to spend the day with the family enjoying the empanada conveyor belt!

INGREDIENTS

For the beef filling

45ml (3 tbsp) olive oil

1 medium onion, diced

2 cloves of garlic, finely chopped

250g minced beef

2 tsp sweet paprika

1 tsp dried oregano

½ tsp ground cumin

2 tsp plain flour

1 tsp sugar

3 tbsp Henderson's Relish

1 egg

Vegetable oil, for frying

A handful of raisins

8 olives, pitted and halved

Salt and pepper, to taste

For the dough

225g plain flour

1 tbsp salt

½ tsp baking powder

150ml warm water

25g lard or vegetable fat, melted (we use Trex)

METHOD

For the beef filling

Heat the oil in the frying pan and sauté the diced onion and garlic over a medium heat for 8-10 minutes until translucent. Turn up the heat and add the beef. Cook while stirring for 5 minutes until the meat is brown. Season the beef mixture with our all-time favourite condiments of sweet paprika, oregano and cumin to form a sofrito. Cook for a further 3 minutes, then add the flour and sugar and cook for another 2 minutes. Remove the pan from the heat, stir in the Henderson's Relish and then leave the mixture to cool. Meanwhile, hard-boil the egg. Once cooled, peel and cut into 8 wedges.

For the dough

Add the flour, salt, baking powder, and water to a large bowl or a stand mixer. Combine until you have crumbs, then add the melted lard or vegetable fat and mix on low speed to form the dough, running the mixer until the dough is soft and flexible. If needed, keep adding water. Once done, separate the dough into 8-10 portions and cover with a moist cloth.

To assemble and cook the empanadas

Heat the vegetable oil to 180°c/350°F in a frying pan. Get a little bowl of water ready and grab a fork, ready to seal the empanadas. While the oil is heating up, roll out your dough balls on a lightly floured surface to a thickness of around 5mm.

Fill each round of dough with 2 tablespoons of your filling, then add a few raisins, a wedge of hard-boiled egg, and a halved olive in the middle. Dip a finger in the water and wet the outside rim of the dough, then fold it over the filling and seal. Pick up the empanada and set aside on a chopping board. Crimp the sealed edge with the prongs of the fork. If you are good at making empanadas, you can do this assembly line style to make and fry them at the same time. If you are just starting out, you probably want to make at least half of the empanadas before you start frying.

When you are ready, slip a few empanadas into the hot oil, bottom side down. Usually, only a small amount of the top of the empanada will bob above the surface of the oil. Fry for 2-3 minutes until golden, then flip. When both sides are golden brown, move the empanada to the cooling rack in the oven and continue with the rest of the empanadas.

CHILEAN

LA MAMA
ZAPALLITOS RELLENOS (STUFFED COURGETTES)

PREPARATION TIME: 15-20 MINUTES // COOKING TIME: 45-50 MINUTES // SERVES 4

Every Chilean home has its own version of this long-standing family favourite. So, here is ours... with a touch of Hendo's, of course!

INGREDIENTS

2 large courgettes

30ml (2 tbsp) olive oil

1 large onion, diced

2-3 cloves of garlic, finely chopped

1 tsp dried oregano

1 tsp ground cumin

Salt and pepper, to taste

2 tbsp Henderson's Relish

675g minced beef

2 eggs

4 tbsp freshly grated Manchego cheese

METHOD

Wash the courgettes and trim off the ends. Place them in a pan of salted cold water, bring to a simmer and cook for 5-10 minutes, until the flesh is tender but still firm.

Remove the courgettes from the pan and set aside until cool enough to handle, then halve them lengthways and use a spoon to remove all the white flesh from the centre, creating a hollow. Reserve the flesh for later. Be careful not to break or split the skin as you prepare the courgettes.

Preheat the oven to 180°c/350°F/Gas Mark 4. In a large pan, heat the oil over a medium heat. Add the garlic, onion, oregano, cumin, salt, and pepper to the pan and fry for 10 minutes, until the onion has softened.

Stir the Henderson's Relish and minced beef into the onion mixture and cook for about 10 minutes until the meat has turned brown. Remove the pan from the heat.

Mash the reserved courgette flesh with a fork and add it to the pan, then quickly stir in the eggs until everything is combined.

Spoon the minced beef mixture into the prepared courgettes, then sprinkle the Manchego cheese on top and add a splash more Hendo's.

Place the stuffed courgettes on a baking sheet and cook in the preheated oven for 15-20 minutes, until the cheese is golden.

CHILEAN

FRANZ VON

JAMAICAN BROWN STEW CHICKEN

PREPARATION TIME: 10-15 MINUTES, PLUS 8 HOURS MARINATING // COOKING TIME: 40-45 MINUTES // SERVES 3-4

Brown stew chicken with white rice or rice and peas is one of my favourite meals. It's a very popular dish in Jamaica. I always look forward to Sunday dinners, which is when this is traditionally served.

INGREDIENTS

½ a chicken, cut into small pieces

4-5 tbsp cooking oil

For the marinade

1 onion, chopped

2 spring onions, chopped

2 cloves of garlic, crushed

¼ scotch bonnet, finely chopped and deseeded

4g fresh ginger, grated

4 sprigs of fresh thyme

2 tbsp browning sauce

2 tbsp soy sauce

2 tbsp all-purpose seasoning

1 tbsp allspice seasoning

1 tbsp chicken seasoning

½ tbsp salt, or to taste

½ tbsp paprika

For the sauce

2 small tomatoes, chopped

1 large carrot, diced

¼ red bell pepper, sliced

¼ green bell pepper, sliced

1 chicken stock cube

2 tbsp tomato ketchup

2 tbsp Henderson's Relish

400ml water (approx.)

METHOD

First, wash the chicken pieces and remove the skin (this step is optional). Shake or pat the chicken dry and then combine it with all the ingredients for the marinade in a large bowl or pan.

Mix it all together and rub the seasoning into the chicken pieces. Cover the bowl or pan with cling film and place in the fridge to marinate overnight so that the flavours can really sink into the meat. If you are pushed for time, then leave it to marinate for 1-2 hours.

When you are ready to cook, remove the chicken from the marinade, saving the marinade in a separate bowl to add later.

Heat the cooking oil in a large pot on a medium to high heat. Fry the chicken on each side for about 3 minutes. Remove the chicken once golden brown.

Prepare the sauce by adding all the ingredients and the reserved marinade to the pot used for browning the chicken on a medium to high heat.

When the sauce starts to boil, add the chicken back into the pot. Cover and leave to simmer for 10-15 minutes. The aim is to cook the browned chicken pieces in a savoury and spicy vegetable sauce which is thickened with the stock cube, ketchup and Henderson's Relish. You may need more or less water than the approximate amount given to get the right consistency.

When the chicken is cooked through and the stew is the right consistency for you, taste to check the seasoning and then serve with boiled white rice or rice and peas.

CARIBBEAN

FRANZ VON

JAMAICAN STEAMED CABBAGE

PREPARATION TIME: 10 MINUTES // COOKING TIME: 10-15 MINUTES // SERVES 3-4

Steamed cabbage takes little time to prepare and cook. It is a healthy, high fibre, low fat dish that's suitable for vegetarians and vegans, and it tastes great. Steamed cabbage is usually served as a side dish and shares a similar reputation to Henderson's Relish as the perfect accompaniment to almost any savoury meal.

INGREDIENTS

3 tbsp cooking oil

1 medium onion

2 cloves of garlic

1 spring onion

½ red bell pepper

½ yellow bell pepper

½ green bell pepper

4 sprigs of fresh thyme

¼ scotch bonnet

2 carrots

1 medium white cabbage

3 tbsp Henderson's Relish

1 tbsp all-purpose seasoning

¼ tbsp salt, or to taste

¼ tbsp black pepper

1 tbsp dairy-free butter

METHOD

First, prepare your ingredients. Peel and chop the onion, peel and finely chop the garlic, slice the spring onion, and dice the peppers. Cut the carrots into thin strips (julienne) and finely chop the scotch bonnet, removing the seeds. Shred the cabbage and set everything aside.

Add the oil to a saucepan or frying pan on a medium heat. Once hot, sauté the onion, garlic and spring onion for 2 minutes. Add the bell peppers, thyme and scotch bonnet to sauté for another 2 minutes, releasing all the flavours ready for them to be absorbed by the cabbage.

Next, add the carrots and sauté for 2 minutes before stirring the shredded cabbage into the other vegetables along with the Henderson's Relish, all-purpose seasoning, salt, and black pepper.

Add the dairy-free butter to the pan and let it melt, tossing or stirring the vegetables to coat them. Give the mixture a good stir and then cover with a lid or tin foil.

Allow the cabbage to steam for 8 to 10 minutes or until the liquid has reduced, then serve and enjoy.

CARIBBEAN

AUSTRALASIA

Travelling further than possibly ever before on our Hendo's world tour, our next chapter treats you to some Aussie and Kiwi classics courtesy of Pom Kitchen and Tamper, both bringing bonzer brunch and other daytime delicacies to the people of Sheffield. If you haven't tried a pie floater or mince on toast before, now's your chance!

TAMPER

TAMPER'S MINCE ON TOAST WITH POACHED EGGS & PICKLES

PREPARATION TIME: 15-20 MINUTES // COOKING TIME: 1-2 HOURS, BUT THE LONGER THE BETTER // SERVES 6-8

A very popular dish at Tamper Coffee that's been on the menu since day one. Tamper's Mince on Toast revolves around using leftover mince from the night before to make a quick breakfast or lunch that is jazzed up a bit with some tasty toppings.

INGREDIENTS

For the mince

1 white onion, finely diced

1 medium carrot, peeled and grated

1 small sweet potato, peeled and grated

1 red pepper, deseeded and diced

Olive oil

4 cloves of garlic, minced

1kg beef mince (we use 10% fat)

75ml Henderson's Relish

125ml red wine

400ml tinned chopped tomatoes

30g or 1 large tbsp black treacle

1 tbsp chipotle chilli paste

1 tbsp ground paprika

A good pinch of salt and pepper

For the toast and toppings

50ml white wine vinegar

6-8 fresh free-range eggs

Any type of bread (we use a fresh ciabatta but focaccia is amazing too)

Pickles of your choice (such as shallots, piccalilli, red cabbage)

METHOD

In a big saucepan, sweat the onion, carrot, sweet potato, and red pepper in a little oil. Once the ingredients are soft and the onions are translucent, add the garlic and cook for a further 2-3 minutes, then remove from the heat and set aside.

In a large frying pan, brown off the mince in 500g batches, making sure you break it up (chef's tip — use a whisk to do this). Once the mince is browned, add it to the pan of vegetables and stir well. When all the meat is mixed in with the vegetables, add the remaining ingredients and bring to a boil.

Turn the heat down to a simmer and cook the mince mixture for a further 1 and a half to 2 hours, making sure to stir occasionally and check the seasoning. When the mince is lovely and soft, start to think about your toast and poached eggs.

Bring a deep pan of water and the white wine vinegar to the boil. When the water is boiling, carefully crack your eggs into the pan. You may only want to do 4 eggs at a time (if it's a small saucepan, swirl the water before dropping in the eggs). Poached eggs normally take around 2 minutes 30 seconds, so slice and toast the bread when you start the eggs. When the eggs are cooked with soft yolks, carefully take them out of the pan with a slotted spoon and drain.

To serve

At Tamper Coffee, we serve our mince on toast with our signature yuzu hollandaise. To enjoy it at home, place your toast on a plate or in a pasta bowl, add a few big spoonfuls of the mince and then top with the poached eggs. Add some pickles of your choice and maybe an extra dash of Hendo's, then tuck in!

NEW ZEALAND

TAMPER

MIXED MUSHROOM GNOCCHI WITH HENDERSON'S CREAM

PREPARATION TIME: 10-15 MINUTES // COOKING TIME: 15-20 MINUTES // SERVES 2-3

This dish is great in autumn or winter: rich and creamy but with enough Henderson's Relish to cut through and create a delicious balance of flavours. Feel free to use a vegan alternative to the cream and butter, and whatever mushrooms you can get hold of (we like wild, chestnut and portobello).

INGREDIENTS

150g chestnut mushrooms

300g other mushrooms (such as wild, flat, oyster, enoki, king)

3-4 cloves of garlic

1 banana shallot or small white onion

150g kale or cavolo nero

Olive oil

50g butter

2 sprigs of thyme, leaves picked

400-500g fresh or homemade gnocchi

20ml Henderson's Relish

50ml white wine (optional)

300g double cream

8-10 sage leaves, roughly chopped

200g cooked chestnuts, chopped (use the vac-packed ones in the supermarket)

Salt and pepper

METHOD

Prepare all your mushrooms by brushing any soil off and slicing them however you like, thinly or chunky. Thinly slice the garlic, finely dice the shallot and chop the kale into 2cm strips.

Place a large frying pan on a medium heat. Add the oil and sweat the shallots for 5 minutes. When the shallots have softened and are golden, add the butter and all the prepared mushrooms, along with the garlic and thyme leaves. Keep on a medium-high heat and stir until the mushrooms are golden on the edge and reduced in size, about 5 minutes. Transfer them to a bowl and return the pan to the heat.

Add a bit more butter to the pan and fry the gnocchi until they are lightly golden brown. Add the mushrooms back to the pan and mix everything well, keeping the heat high. Add the Henderson's Relish and white wine if using. Stir for a minute, making sure you don't fully reduce the liquids.

Pour in the cream and mix everything together. Let it come to a boil, then lower the heat and stir in the kale along with half the sage leaves. The kale will take 2-3 minutes to cook through. When this is done, check the seasoning and maybe add a bit more Henderson's if you like.

Share the mushroom gnocchi between pasta bowls, then top with the chopped chestnuts and a few fresh sage leaves. At Tamper, we like to garnish this with crispy sage and fried enoki mushrooms.

Chef's Tip: Get everything prepared and to hand before you start the cooking process. If you are cooking for more people and increasing quantities, it may be worth blanching the gnocchi in boiling water first, then draining it well before pan frying.

NEW ZEALAND

ROAST APPLE & HENDERSON'S CARAMEL FRENCH TOAST

PREPARATION TIME: 30-45 MINUTES // COOKING TIME: 10-15 MINUTES // SERVES 4

French toast is a very popular dish at Tamper. We love to change it up, and this is a Sheffield favourite! Use brioche or other bread that's a bit old and stale, which avoids waste and helps it soak up all the flavours. If you haven't got time to make the gingernut crumble, just crush up some gingerbread men or gingernut biscuits instead.

INGREDIENTS

For the Hendo's caramel
150g caster sugar

150g double cream

20g unsalted butter

20ml Henderson's Relish

For the vanilla sour cream
1 tsp vanilla paste or essence

200g sour cream

For the gingernut crumble
150g plain flour

50g porridge oats

80g butter

50g brown sugar

½ tbsp ground ginger

½ tsp ground cinnamon

Small pinch of salt

For the French toast
2 Granny Smith apples, peeled and cubed

80g light brown or demerara sugar

3 medium free-range eggs

100g double cream

1 tsp ground cinnamon

1 brioche loaf, cut into 4 x 2.5cm slices

1 punnet of blueberries (150-200g)

METHOD

For the Hendo's caramel
Place the caster sugar and 2 tablespoons of water into a large saucepan and mix to a paste. Place this on a high heat and bring to a boil, making sure you have the cream, butter and Henderson's Relish measured out and ready to add. The sugar should start to boil rapidly and slowly start to brown. When the browning begins, softly shake the pan (do not stir!) and watch the colour carefully. When it is evenly golden, turn the heat off. Slowly and carefully whisk in the cream, butter and Henderson's Relish. Watch out as this will create a lot of steam. When all the ingredients are fully incorporated, set the caramel aside to cool.

For the vanilla sour cream
In a bowl, simply mix the vanilla into the sour cream. Store in the fridge until needed.

For the gingernut crumble
Preheat the oven to 170°c. Place all the ingredients into a large bowl or food processor and mix to a rough crumb. Spread this out on a lined baking tray and place in the oven for 20-25 minutes. After 10-12 minutes, give the crumb a stir. Cook until golden, then remove and leave to cool.

For the French toast
Add a generous knob of butter to a saucepan and place on a high heat. When the butter starts to foam, add the apples and stir well. After 3-5 minutes, they should have softened. Add the sugar, turn the heat down low and cook for a further 5 minutes. Meanwhile, mix the eggs, cream and cinnamon in a shallow bowl. Dip and soak your brioche slices in this mixture. Preheat the oven to 180°c. Place a large frying pan on a medium-high heat with some oil and a generous knob of butter. When the butter starts to foam, add the soaked brioche and start frying. Keep on a medium-high heat and cook for 2 minutes or so, then check and flip over to cook the other side. When both sides are golden-brown, place in the oven for 5-8 minutes.

To serve
Scatter the gingernut crumb over the plate, add the French toast and top with a few spoonfuls of roast apple. Scatter blueberries around the plate, add a dollop of vanilla sour cream on the side, and drizzle your Hendo's caramel on top.

NEW ZEALAND

DRUNKEN HENDERSON'S NOODLES

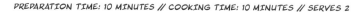

PREPARATION TIME: 10 MINUTES // COOKING TIME: 10 MINUTES // SERVES 2

These noodles are a super quick and easy nod to the huge Pan Asian influence in Aussie cooking. The addition of Henderson's Relish adds a real depth to the lip-smackingly spicy sauce!

INGREDIENTS

1 packet of dried flat rice noodles

3 red bird's eye chillies (or more if you can handle it!)

4 cloves of garlic, peeled

1 tbsp vegetable oil

1 packet of firm tofu, cut into large chunks

1 tsp dark soy sauce

1 tsp light soy sauce

1 tsp Henderson's Relish

1 tbsp brown or palm sugar

Handful of green beans, halved

Broccoli or green veg of your choice

Generous handful of baby corn, halved

Lots of chopped Thai basil

METHOD

Cook the noodles according to the packet instructions. Meanwhile, use a pestle and mortar to pound the chillies and garlic together to form a rough paste.

Heat the veg oil in a wok over a high heat. Add your chilli-garlic paste and stir-fry for 30 seconds until fragrant, then add the flat noodles to the pan and stir-fry for 1 minute until coated with the paste.

Add the tofu, dark soy sauce, light soy sauce, Henderson's Relish, and sugar to the pan. Mix well to combine everything, stir-fry for 30 seconds, then add your veg and a generous handful of Thai basil.

Stir-fry the mixture for about 2 minutes, until the vegetables are just cooked through. Remove from the heat and serve straight away with more Thai basil, a squeeze of lime juice, and fresh sliced chilli if you dare!

AUSTRALIAN

POM KITCHEN

AUSSIE STYLE MUSHROOM PIE FLOATER

PREPARATION TIME: 15-20 MINUTES // COOKING TIME: 1 HOUR // SERVES 4

A pie floater is classic Australian tucker! Typically a meat pie served upside down in a bowl of mushy peas with ketchup, our Pom Mushroom Pie is a vegan take on this delicious Aussie comfort food.

INGREDIENTS

2 packs of ready-rolled puff pastry

500g mixed mushrooms

75g vegan butter

4 tbsp olive oil

4 cloves of garlic, minced

3 medium white onions, finely chopped

3 sticks of celery, finely chopped

1 carrot, finely chopped

½ a small swede, diced

200ml white wine

300ml soy cream

3 tsp Dijon mustard

2 tbsp Henderson's Relish

Handful of chopped fresh flat leaf parsley

1 tbsp oat milk, mixed with 1 tsp olive oil

METHOD

First, blind bake your pie crust. Grease your pie dish well and line it with the pastry. Prick the base all over with a fork to remove any air pockets, then cover your pastry with baking paper and fill with baking beans or uncooked rice. Be sure to leave enough pastry for a lid.

Put the pie dish in a preheated oven at 200°c for 10-12 minutes until the pastry has begun to colour. Remove it, take out the baking paper and beans, then pop the pastry back into the oven for a further 10 minutes until light golden and dry to touch. Allow the pastry case to cool before filling it.

Divide the mushrooms into 4 batches so you can cook easily! Divide your butter into 5 portions, then add one portion to a frying pan along with 1 tablespoon of the olive oil and the first batch of mushrooms. Cook the mushrooms, stirring occasionally, until golden and starting to crisp on the edges. Season lightly, set the first batch aside and then repeat with the remaining mushrooms, butter and oil.

Meanwhile, melt the last portion of butter in a saucepan suitable for a stew or soup. Add the garlic, onion, celery, carrot, and swede. Cook everything over a gentle heat until starting to soften and the onion is becoming translucent.

Now add all your cooked mushrooms to the pan along with the white wine. Bring to the boil, then turn down the heat and simmer until nearly all the liquid has gone. Add the soy cream, mustard, Henderson's Relish, and chopped parsley, then season well with salt and pepper.

Spoon the mushroom mixture into your blind baked pie crust, add a pastry lid and then brush all the exposed pastry with the oat milk and olive oil wash.

Pop your pie into the oven and bake at 190°c for about 30-45 minutes until golden and smelling delicious! Serve with a mound of buttery mash on top, plus mushy peas and gravy with red sauce (aka ketchup) on the side for true Aussie vibes!

AUSTRALIAN

AFRICA & THE MIDDLE EAST

Our final stops take in the cuisines of South Africa, Egypt and Turkey to conclude the gastronomic globetrotting of Henderson's Relish. Chuck some chicken wings on the braai, transport your tastebuds to Cairo with a warming torley, and try a vegetarian take on a famous Turkish dish alongside the talented chefs who are blending the food of their heritage with South Yorkshire's much-loved condiment, proving that Hendo's really can do it all when it comes to culinary creativity.

ORANGE BIRD
MONKEY GLAND PORK NECK & WHIPPED GARLIC

PREPARATION TIME: 1 HOUR // COOKING TIME: 20 MINUTES // SERVES 2

No monkeys required — the origins of the sauce in this South African dish are debated and worth a Google, but essentially it's a deliciously sweet sauce used to marinate meat, or served on the side as you would with a barbecue sauce. Make a big batch and use it on everything!

INGREDIENTS

2 x 150g pork neck steaks

For the monkey gland sauce

20ml vegetable oil

1 red onion, finely diced

2 cloves of garlic, minced

1 tsp thyme leaves

1 tsp cayenne

1 tsp hot smoked paprika

250g ketchup

50g apricot jam

30ml Henderson's Relish

20g good plum chutney

15g sugar

10g soy sauce

1 tsp Dijon mustard

For the whipped garlic

135g garlic, peeled and germ removed

2 tsp Maldon salt

1 tsp Dijon mustard

60ml lemon juice

60ml cold water

600ml vegetable oil

METHOD

For the monkey gland sauce

Heat the oil in a pan and sauté the red onion until softened and slightly coloured, then add the garlic, thyme, cayenne and paprika. Continue to cook for 3 minutes, then add 100ml of water and all the remaining ingredients. Reduce the volume of liquid by a quarter, then leave the sauce to cool.

For the whipped garlic

Place the garlic, salt and mustard in a food processor, pulse to a paste and then add about 10ml of the lemon juice, followed by roughly 50ml of the oil. Continue to alternate these additions until all the lemon juice has been incorporated, then alternate the oil with the cold water until combined.

For the pork

Coat the pork with a fifth of the monkey gland sauce (reserve the rest to serve alongside) and a little Maldon salt, and then leave it to rest in the fridge for 1 hour.

Remove the pork from the fridge about an hour before cooking, allowing it to reach room temperature. Cook over hot coals or in a cast iron pan on a high heat, until the sauce has caramelised and the meat has a core temperature of 55°c. Once cooked, rest the pork for roughly 10 minutes, during which time it should reach a maximum core temperature of approximately 60°c.

Carve the rested pork, then serve with the whipped garlic and reserved monkey gland sauce.

SOUTH AFRICAN

ORANGE BIRD

JAN P BOOYENS' CHICKEN WINGS

PREPARATION TIME: 5 MINUTES, PLUS 1 HOUR TO MARINATE // COOKING TIME: 1 HOUR // SERVES 4-6

A customer suggested this recipe to us while visiting the restaurant; it's a favourite of his family in South Africa and was dreamt up by his dad in the 1960s to form part of their family braai. It was an immediate hit with our family and friends, with the addition of Henderson's Relish of course!

INGREDIENTS

1.5kg large chicken wings

352g All Gold Tomato Sauce

136g Mrs Balls Original Chutney

30ml Henderson's Relish

Salt and pepper

METHOD

Place the chicken wings in a pan and cover with water. Bring to a simmer, skimming any scum off the top, and simmer for 35 minutes, until tender. Drain and cool.

Combine the tomato sauce, chutney, and Henderson's Relish to make the marinade. Add salt and pepper to taste, cover the cooled chicken wings in the marinade, then leave for at least an hour.

Finish the marinated chicken wings on a hot braai (barbecue) for 5-10 minutes until piping hot, crispy and irresistible!

SOUTH
AFRICAN

ORANGE BIRD

FANCY WINTER POTJIE

PREPARATION TIME: 10 MINUTES // COOKING TIME: 3-4 HOURS // SERVES 8-10

The ultimate stew, cooked in a large cast-iron three-legged pot (potjie pot) over warm coals. This is such a great example of South African cuisine: nourishing, hearty and a real mix of cultures, from Cape Malay spices to the tougher cuts of meat cooked over fire in a pot brought from the Netherlands. Social gatherings always call for either a braai or a potjie and they're always delicious.

INGREDIENTS

500g diced venison

500g diced lamb leg

250g boneless beef short rib, diced

½ tsp crushed coriander seeds

½ tsp curry powder

½ tsp paprika

½ tsp Maldon salt

60ml olive oil

2 red onions, finely diced

6 cloves of garlic, crushed

1 litre beef stock

1 litre red wine

1 tbsp honey

2 tbsp thyme leaves

½ tsp ground allspice

½ tsp ground cinnamon

400g good quality tinned tomatoes

50ml Henderson's Relish

3 carrots, peeled and cut into large chunks

1 butternut squash, peeled and cut into chunks

METHOD

Coat the diced meat evenly in the coriander, curry powder, paprika, and salt. Heat the olive oil in a potjie pot (preferably over warm coals) and then cook the onion and garlic until coloured.

Add the venison, lamb, and beef to the pot and cook until brown. Once coloured, add the beef stock, red wine, honey, thyme, allspice, cinnamon, tinned tomatoes, Henderson's Relish, carrots, and squash. Cover with a lid and cook slowly (without stirring) for 2.5 to 3 hours until the meat is tender.

Once the potjie is done, taste the sauce to check the seasoning and then finish with a little chutney of your choice (we use Mrs Balls Original Chutney) for sweetness before serving.

SOUTH AFRICAN

SEYOUF KITCHEN OF KOSHARI STREET

STREET CHICKEN SHAWARMA

PREPARATION TIME: 5 MINUTES, PLUS TIME TO MARINATE // COOKING TIME: 15 MINUTES // SERVES 3-4

Probably the most succulent way to cook your chicken thighs while extracting the most flavour from them. This summery dish is perfect with bread rolls or a fresh green salad with pomegranate seeds.

INGREDIENTS

400g boneless chicken thighs

250g Greek yoghurt

2 cloves of garlic, crushed

1 red onion, diced

1 lemon, juiced

10g Henderson's Relish

10g black pepper

5g paprika

5g ground turmeric

5g chicken spice or allspice

2g onion powder

1g ground cumin

METHOD

Cut the chicken thighs into thin slices and place them in a deep bowl with all the other ingredients. Stir well and then leave to marinate for at least 1 hour (bonus points for 3-6 hours marinating).

When you're ready to cook, heat up a large Teflon or well-seasoned cast iron pan, or a wok, and then add the marinated chicken in a single even layer, making sure all the meat is in contact with the pan's surface.

Let the chicken sizzle on one side without moving it for 2 minutes until golden brown, then stir fry for 10 minutes on a high heat.

Test a piece to see if the chicken is cooked through, then leave it on low heat for a final 5 minutes. Add water if necessary to loosen the sauce for your preferred consistency.

Turn the heat off and serve the chicken with its sauce, adding a few drops of Henderson's Relish for extra flavour if you like. The finished shawarma is best served in a soft bread roll with green lettuce, kale, and coriander sauce.

Chef's Tip: Leave the chicken to marinate for 3-6 hours in the fridge for best results.

EGYPTIAN

BEEF HALLA CASSEROLE

PREPARATION TIME: 10 MINUTES // COOKING TIME: 3-4 HOURS // SERVES 3-4

This rich dish is traditionally home cooked in a zalata, a large stone pot that retains and distributes heat like no other. It packs in a ton of flavour as a result of three to four hours of slow cooking and braising and is usually served with plain white Egyptian rice to soak up the thick beef gravy.

INGREDIENTS

500g beef (chuck, shoulder, or casserole cut)

1 white onion

3 cloves of garlic

10g salt

5g black pepper

2g paprika

2g ground coriander

1g ground cumin

1g onion powder

25g olive oil

10g Henderson's Relish

Fresh coriander, to garnish

METHOD

Slice the beef into 2-3mm steaks (or ask the butcher to do this for you) and then salt generously. Set the steaks aside for 2 minutes while you halve and slice the onion, then peel and finely chop the garlic (without making it into a paste). Combine all the dry spices in a small bowl.

Pour the olive oil into a deep casserole on a high heat. Once hot, add the beef steaks and fry for 3 minutes per side until browned and seared. Transfer them to a plate and set aside to rest.

Add the onion and garlic to the hot oil, stir for 1 minute, then place the beef steaks back in the pot. Add the spice mix and Henderson's Relish, stir to ensure everything is well mixed, then add hot water until the beef steaks are just covered.

Cover the pot and leave on a low heat for 45 minutes, then add more water to cover the beef steaks again. Repeat this step three times, so you have added water and braised four times in total, then take the pot off the heat once the beef is soft and the sauce is thick. Test whether the steaks are cooked by prodding them with a fork, which should go in easily.

Chop some fresh coriander and garnish your beef casserole with it to serve.

EGYPTIAN

CAIRO TORLEY MINCE & VEGETABLE STEW

PREPARATION TIME: 5 MINUTES // COOKING TIME: 45 MINUTES // SERVES 3-4

A family favourite, this vegetable and beef mince stew is traditionally prepared in massive casserole pots to feed large families in winter months. It combines the sweetness of carrots and starchy potatoes with umami beef flavour for the ultimate comfort food and is typically served with Egyptian bread or other types of flatbreads.

INGREDIENTS

2 tomatoes

2 large carrots

2 large potatoes

2 medium red onions

3 cloves of garlic, peeled

70g butter

5g salt

10g black pepper

10g Henderson's Relish

500g beef mince (15% fat)

400g green peas (frozen or fresh)

1 chicken, beef or vegetable stock cube

Fresh parsley, to garnish

METHOD

Dice the tomatoes and slice the carrots. Peel the potatoes if preferred, then cut into bite-size cubes. Peel and finely dice the onions, then finely chop the garlic (without making it into a paste).

Place a large casserole on a high heat and melt the butter. Add the onions and garlic with the salt and pepper, then stir in the beef mince and cook until it has browned, and the onions are soft.

Add half the Henderson's Relish to the beef mixture, then top with the tomatoes, carrots, potatoes, and peas in an even layer. Pour in 250ml of hot water, or enough to cover all the ingredients, then add the remaining Henderson's Relish and crumble in the stock cube.

Cover the pot and leave on a low heat for 45 minutes, then try the potatoes and carrots to see if they're cooked through. Once the stew is ready, leave it to rest off the heat for 20 minutes.

Garnish the finished stew with chopped fresh parsley and serve in a soup bowl with flatbreads.

Chef's Tip: Add 2 scotch bonnet peppers near the end of the cooking time to bring out the spiciness of the dish.

EGYPTIAN

MAVI RUYA

HENDO'S SPECIAL

PREPARATION TIME: 10 MINUTES // COOKING TIME: 5-10 MINUTES // SERVES 1-2

This dish celebrates both Anatolian cuisine and Yorkshire heritage, where the two worlds collide at our restaurant in South Yorkshire. It's about past and present: traditional Turkish recipes and great sauces that both make delicious homemade dishes for all generations.

INGREDIENTS

180g boneless chicken breasts

2 tbsp olive oil

10g butter

50g Spanish onion, finely chopped

1 clove of garlic, finely chopped

8 green beans, trimmed

3 mushrooms, diced

1 tbsp Henderson's Relish

2 tbsp double cream

1 tbsp black pepper

1 tbsp oregano

1 tbsp salt

METHOD

Preheat a pan until you can feel the heat by holding your hand 4-5cm above the surface (or if you have a laser thermometer, you can check when the surface temperature reaches 185°c). Season the chicken with salt and pepper, then place in the pan with the oil and cook over a medium heat for 4 minutes on each side. Once the chicken is cooked through, take it out the pan and set aside to rest.

Using the same pan, melt the butter and begin to sauté the onion and garlic. When they are starting to turn golden brown, add the green beans and mushrooms.

Once the beans and mushrooms are tender, add the Henderson's Relish, double cream, black pepper, oregano, and salt. Mix well and then place the chicken breasts back into the pan.

Simmer until the sauce has thickened and the chicken is piping hot. Taste and season with more salt, pepper, and oregano if needed. Serve hot and enjoy!

TURKISH

MAVI RUYA

KABAK SPECIAL

PREPARATION TIME: 30 MINUTES // COOKING TIME: 10 MINUTES // SERVES 1-2

Bursting with aromatic spices and succulent courgettes, this vegetarian delight is the perfect alternative for those craving a memorable dining experience. Our recipe was inspired by Islim Kebab, one of the most famous Turkish dishes, which originated in the city of Gaziantep but is made with slight variations all over Turkey.

INGREDIENTS

1 large courgette, cut into wide strips

2 medium aubergines, peeled and cubed

1 green, yellow, and red bell pepper, deseeded and quartered

2 cloves of garlic, finely diced

½ tbsp red pepper flakes

½ tbsp black pepper

½ tbsp salt

4 tbsp rapeseed oil

¼ Spanish onion, finely diced

3 tbsp tomato paste

200ml water

1 tbsp Henderson's Relish

Handful of grated cheese (optional)

Handful of chopped flat leaf parsley

METHOD

Preheat the oven to 250°c. Place the courgette strips into a frying pan on a medium heat with 2 tablespoons of the rapeseed oil and roast for about 7 minutes, turning them occasionally with metal tongs. Cook until the skin is charred and the flesh is soft, then transfer the courgette strips to a colander and allow to cool.

Mix the prepared aubergine and bell pepper with the garlic, red pepper flakes, black pepper, and salt in a large bowl. Toss to combine everything thoroughly, cover and set aside.

Heat the remaining rapeseed oil in the frying pan (it should be enough to cover the base) and sauté the Spanish onion until light golden and soft. Add the tomato paste and cook over a low heat. The consistency should be light yet thick enough to coat your wooden spoon.

Once the tomato paste and onion have mixed and started to thicken, turn the heat down and gradually add the water, stirring continually to keep the consistency smooth.

Add the seasoned aubergine and peppers to the pan and mix thoroughly. Check the seasoning, add more salt and black pepper to taste if needed, then stir in the Henderson's Relish. Once everything is well combined and cooked through, set the pan to one side.

Prepare an ovenproof metal or clay pan as shown in the picture and lay the cooled courgette strips in the pan like a flower, starting from the centre and working outwards. Spoon the aubergine mixture into the centre of each strip, then roll or fold the courgette into a little parcel around the filling.

If you like, sprinkle the courgette parcels with grated cheese once they are all done. Place the pan in the preheated oven for 7 minutes, then serve with a sprinkle of fresh parsley on top. Enjoy!

TURKISH

MAVI RUYA

TURKISH LAMB PIDE

PREPARATION TIME: 40-45 MINUTES // COOKING TIME: 15 MINUTES // SERVES 2-3

Turkish pide (pronounced as pee-DEH) is a delicious savoury flatbread formed into a boat-like shape. They can be filled with a variety of fresh ingredients and make a comforting meal in themselves.

INGREDIENTS

For the dough

300ml warm water

4g yeast

750g plain or self-raising flour

1 tsp salt

2 tbsp olive oil

For the filling

3 cloves of garlic, finely diced

300g lamb, cut into small cubes

2 mixed bell peppers, finely diced

2 tbsp Henderson's Relish

Salt and black pepper, to taste

Chilli flakes, to taste

METHOD

For the dough

In a bowl or stand mixer, combine the warm water and yeast. Stir and then set aside, allowing the mixture to bloom for 5 minutes until the edges get foamy.

Add the flour and salt to the bloomed yeast, using a wooden spoon to combine everything until you have a soft dough. Transfer this to a clean, well-floured surface and knead for a couple of minutes. You can use additional tablespoons of flour while kneading if needed. The dough should be slightly sticky but soft.

Place the dough in a large bowl and drizzle a little bit of olive oil on top, then cover with plastic wrap and a tea towel. Place the bowl in a warm place and leave to rise for about 30-35 minutes or until doubled in size.

For the filling

While the dough proves, heat a pan and sauté the garlic in olive oil. Add the lamb and cook until almost done, then add the peppers. Once they have softened and the lamb is cooked through, season the mixture with the Henderson's Relish, salt, black pepper and chilli to your liking. Transfer to a plate to cool.

Preheat the oven to 200°c. Once the dough has doubled in size, halve it and cover one half to prevent it drying out while you work with the other half. Place this on a clean surface and stretch out the dough into a boat or canoe-like shape.

Brush the shaped dough with some olive oil and place half the lamb filling in the centre, leaving a border of about 2cm. Now fold the edges of the dough over the filling and pinch or twist the ends. You can use egg wash or olive oil to glaze the pide, brushing it all over the outer dough.

Repeat the steps above to make the second pide, then lift them both carefully onto a pizza stone lined with parchment paper. Bake in the preheated oven for around 10-15 minutes or until lightly golden along the edges. Slice into pieces and enjoy!

TURKISH

EUROPE

GRAZIE

Inspired by traditional flavours, Grazie offers a fresh, creative, and original interpretation of Puglian cuisine. Situated in the heart of Sheffield, the restaurant is passionate about providing fresh homemade Italian food and unique Apulian dishes using local independent suppliers. A particular star is their fresh homemade pasta, crafted each day in their pasta lab.

PUBLIC

Occupying the former gent's toilet below the grade 1 listed Victorian town hall in Sheffield, Public is a tiny haven of fine drinks, or as it was once described, 'a Wes Anderson train carriage crowbarred into an old bog'. Since opening in 2017, Public has scooped up a string of awards including being named as Observer's Best Place to Drink in the UK.

DOG & PARTRIDGE

With a rich history that can be traced back to the Elizabethan period, supplying shelter and refreshments for travellers crossing the hostile moors of the Pennines, the Dog & Partridge is situated on the old medieval salt way route in Sheffield. Today, it serves up locally sourced, hand-pulled cask beers and traditional country cooking.

MOLLY'S CAFÉ

Taking inspiration from travels around the world, Molly's is an award-winning deli serving up an Anglo-Polish fusion menu alongside house blend coffee and cakes, as well as providing a catering service. As a family-run café, Molly's prides itself on delivering high-quality, homemade, locally sourced produce served with a smile.

TWO THIRDS BEER CO.

Two Thirds is an independent craft beer bar, kitchen and bottle shop that also offers German-themed street food hot out of the Holy Schnitz kitchen, seven days a week. The ideal food to pair with beer, it includes irresistible grazing dishes, loaded German dogs, Schnitz Burgers, and topped fries, plus a whole host of vegan options.

IRINI TZORTZOGLOU

Irini Tzortzoglou is a celebrity chef, published author, olive oil and honey sommelier, and motivational speaker. She runs her own culinary retreats in Greece and Cumbria, and has launched her own 'Yiayia' Gin and a series of Greek menus with chef-led recipe box company the Cookaway. Irini is also a regular contributor to Cumbria Life with a monthly restaurant review feature titled 'Irini Eats'.

BARESCA NOTTINGHAM

This tapas restaurant has been bringing Spanish spirit from Barcelona to Byard Lane since 2015, serving authentic tapas dishes from cocos (flatbreads) to tortillas and tacos. With a first floor dining area and atmospheric underground bar as well as the main restaurant, baresca is a slice of the Catalan capital in Nottingham.

JAMESON'S TEAROOM & KITCHEN

Jameson's has been a well-known name in Sheffield since 1883. Originally famous for antiques, the tearoom now prides itself on British afternoon teas, home baked cakes, breakfast, brunches, delightful lunches and a welcoming atmosphere. Ideal for occasions, they also offer takeaway and outside catering for events and parties.

INDIAN SUBCONTINENT

PINDY'S SAMOSAS

Established in 2017, Pindy's Samosas brings delicious, high-quality, Punjabi samosas to your table. Pindy has been making samosas for over twenty years and is passionate about food, especially the ways in which it can bring people together. Hand-crafted from family principles with natural ingredients, each samosa gives you a wonderful experience of texture and flavour that leaves you wanting more!

HUNGRY BUDDHA

Hungry Buddha creates home cooked, fresh and healthy food with authentic flavours from the mountain peaks of Nepal. Founder Dev misses the humble community which sharing food in Nepal creates, offering a taste of this sincerity in the

RUKMINI IYER

Rukmini Iyer is a cookery writer and the author of the bestselling Roasting Tin series. Formerly a lawyer, she now loves creating new minimum fuss, maximum flavour recipes to help busy households. When she's not cooking or entertaining friends, the border collie and the baby, she can usually be found gardening. Her latest book, India Express, is out now.

UK through Hungry Buddha with flavoursome, subtly spiced, Nepalese food at his restaurant within Sheffield's Moor Market.

COLOMBO STREET FOOD

Colombo's mission is to provide a taste of Sri Lanka in the UK, using their team of chefs' traditional family recipes and high quality ingredients to provide the explosion of flavour that is Sri Lankan food. Located in the Sheffield Plate food hall at the heart of Sheffield, Colombo Street Food also has locations in Glossop and Halifax.

TORIE TRUE

Torie True is a food writer, home cook and cookery teacher of Indian food who learnt her craft through travels to India as well as her husband's Indian family. She is passionate about cooking with spices and aims to instil this love and enthusiasm in those who attend her popular Indian cooking classes. Torie writes a food and travel blog (www.chilliandmint.com) as well as articles for a range of food publications and is the author of the 2021 cookbook Chilli & Mint.

ATUL KOCHHAR

Born in Jamshedpur, Atul Kochhar has become a global culinary icon whose inimitable talent as a twice Michelin-starred chef has changed the way people perceive and experience Indian food. Having been at the forefront of the Indian culinary industry for more than 25 years, Atul received his first Michelin star in 2001 while working at Tamarind in London, making him one of the first British-based Indian chefs to receive the accolade. In more recent years, Atul has been developing his own independent ventures, including a group of successful restaurants in London, Kent, Buckinghamshire and Berkshire, plus a bespoke catering company, Amod Events. Atul has also published several admired Indian cookbooks and has become a recognisable face of modern Indian cuisine.

5 TARA

Founder Amanpreet Singh Bawa started 5 Tara with the desire to keep his cultural cuisine alive. He had noticed massive cultural discrepancies in the way traditional Indian flavours have been anglicised, so 5 Tara reinstates these roots in North Indian cuisine, celebrating it in its authentic form.

ASHOKA

Inspired by traditional Indian cuisine, Ashoka was established in 1967 and has been delivering delicious curries to the people of Sheffield ever since. From gloriously tender Kashmiri Lamb to Saag Chicken, Ashoka prides itself on sharing the best Indian cuisine in a warm, friendly atmosphere.

EAST & SOUTHEAST ASIA

CHINA RED

China Red specialises in authentic Szechuan cuisine, celebrating traditional food from the Chinese province with weekly specials and unique experimental dishes in the Sheffield restaurant. If you're looking to add some spice to your life, Szechuan cuisine could be just the thing for you!

GUYSHI

A unique Japanese BBQ restaurant, Guyshi specialises in cooking bite-size meat and vegetables on griddles. Each table has a built-in smokeless roaster to bring people together in an interactive cooking experience and Guyshi also boasts a live teppanyaki station where expert chefs cook a menu of your choice, bringing together food and fun in an exciting atmosphere.

SYIOK LAH

Serving up authentic Malaysian food, Syiok Lah offers vibrant dishes from their food stall at Cutlery Works in Sheffield and pop ups at markets and events around the country. Creating delicious Malaysian dishes from locally sourced ingredients, notably their Halal chicken, Syiok Lah brings this lesser known cuisine into the spotlight.

THE AMERICAS

STREET FOOD CHEF

Street Food Chef is a family-run Mexican street food outlet passionate about providing a healthy fast-food alternative to the people of Sheffield. Best known for their burritos, tacos and quesadillas, they also serve gluten- and dairy-free options. Street Food Chef believes that fast food can taste great, ensuring all the food is freshly prepared every day using locally sourced fresh ingredients.

PIÑA

Born from a summer embarking on the trip of a lifetime around Mexico with a concise to-do list: watching sports, eating tacos, drinking mezcal. Piña specialises in authentic Mexican tacos and refreshing cocktails in an undeniably cool repurposed warehouse in Sheffield's Kelham Island.

UNIT

Prioritising quality, Unit serves traditional burgers and new creations alongside a selection of slow-cooked briskets, waffles and much more. Established in 2016, Unit started out as a creative independent restaurant catering for families and students in Sheffield and has since gone from strength to strength, cooking up mouthwatering American cuisine that customers love.

SHOOT THE BULL

An award-winning catering company, Shoot The Bull are based in Yorkshire and combine their many years of experience with modern innovation. Their chefs have worked in top-notch restaurants across the country, with culinary talents and exciting flavour combinations offering quirky and unrestricted dining experiences for any occasion.

DOMINIQUE WOOLF

Half-Thai Dominique Woolf was the winner of Channel 4's The Great Cookbook Challenge with Jamie Oliver, wowing the judges with her accessible Asian recipes. Her book, Dominique's Kitchen, became a Sunday Times bestseller. Dominique now contributes recipes to magazines such as BBC Good Food and Sainsbury's and has her own food range — The Woolf's Kitchen — of Asian sauces, chilli oils and pastes inspired by those her Thai auntie used to make. Dominique is passionate about sharing her love of big, bold flavours and Asian cuisine. She lives in London with her husband and three little taste testers.

LA MAMA

Established in 2009, La Mama is very proud to cook and serve Latin tapas dishes which draw inspiration from the owner's native homeland of Chile. The menu is inspired by recipes passed down from their abuela and mama, which is the secret to La Mama's unique and award-winning tapas!

FRANZ VON

Franz Von is a Jamaican-born, Sheffield-based musical innovator, afro-fusion artist and emcee who fuses reggae, hip-hop, roots and rap sounds in his work, regularly collaborating with artists in the Steel City and across the UK.

AUSTRALASIA

TAMPER

Bringing Kiwi coffee culture to Sheffield, Tamper is situated in Sellers Wheel, a 19th century former silversmiths in the heart of Sheffield's cultural industries quarter. Offering all day brunch, coffee and good vibes, Tamper creates delicious brunch options from locally sourced, sustainable produce.

POM KITCHEN

More is more, less is a bore! Pom is a plant-based kitchen, café, deli and lifestyle store offering a jam-packed menu of food and drinks for colour enthusiasts and rainbow lovers. Pink and quirky are two of the best words to describe Pom Kitchen, which is anything but minimal and specialises in show-stopping shakes, hot chocolates, and pink bagels.

AFRICA & THE MIDDLE EAST

KOSHARI STREET

Koshari is the most beloved Egyptian street food: heartwarming and healthy, straight from the souks and squares of Cairo. Koshari Street honours this traditional Egyptian dish in all its glory, offering glorious bowls of authentic Egyptian cuisine in multiple London locations.

MAVI RUYA

Mavi Ruya prides itself on offering the finest Anatolian cuisine; with over twenty years' experience of creating mouth-watering dishes and seasonal specials, they have something to suit every palate. Everything from the floor tiles to the light fittings are sourced from Turkey, creating a unique way to experience traditional Turkish culture in Sheffield.

ORANGE BIRD

Orange Bird is a neighbourhood restaurant in the heart of Hillsborough. Their food combines modern South African cuisine with international influences, cooking up delicious dishes on a Braai for guests to enjoy alongside a selection of exquisite drinks. Orange Bird was a runner-up in the 2022 Observer Food Monthly awards and featured in the 2023 Good Food Guide's Top 100 Best Local Restaurants.

Hendo's vs The World

©2023 Henderson's Relish &
Meze Publishing Limited

First edition printed in 2023
in the UK

ISBN: 978-1-915538-21-5

Compiled by: Katie Fisher,
Nick Hallam & Emma Toogood

Written by: Katie Fisher

Spiced Mushroom, Pistachio & Cranberry
Biryani Pie
Crispy Loaded Fries with Masala
Chickpeas & Coriander Chutney
Chilli, Cheese & Potato Stuffed Parathas
Copyright © Rukmini Iyer 2023

Photography by: Paul Gregory
& Marc Barker

Dominique Woolf Portrait by
Lisa Gilby

Torie True Portrait by Tim Green

Irini Tzortzoglou Portrait by Focus
Pocus, Heraklion, Crete

Atul Kochhar's portrait by Kanishka
Portraits

Orange Bird Portrait by Ellie Grace

Designed by: Paul Cocker,
Vicky Frost & Phil Turner

Sales & Marketing: Emma Toogood, Lizzy
Capps

Printed and bound in the UK by
Bell & Bain Ltd, Glasgow

Published by Meze Publishing Limited
Unit 1b, 2 Kelham Square
Kelham Riverside
Sheffield S3 8SD
Web: www.mezepublishing.co.uk
Telephone: 0114 275 7709
Email: info@mezepublishing.co.uk